THE MUCKRAKERS AND AMERICAN SOCIETY

Problems in American Civilization

The
MUCKRAKERS
AND AMERICAN SOCIETY

EDITED WITH AN INTRODUCTION BY

Herbert Shapiro

UNIVERSITY OF CINCINNATI

D. C. HEATH AND COMPANY · Boston
A division of RAYTHEON EDUCATION COMPANY

Library of Congress Catalog Card Number: 68-19015

COPYRIGHT © 1968 BY RAYTHEON EDUCATION COMPANY

INTRODUCTION

DURING the course of American history journalism has significantly influenced the nation's politics and culture. Sometimes journalists have appealed to popular prejudices or have placed the profit motive above serving the public interest; but American journalism also has its reform tradition, its heritage of writers who have sought to make the promise of democracy a living reality. Jeffersonian theory asserted that an educated, informed public was the basis of democracy. An enlightened citizenry requires accurate information; crusading journalists have worked to fulfill that need. The modern journalist who relates his writings to some objective of social improvement can find precedent for his efforts in the work of propagandists who furthered the American Revolution, or in the attempt of abolitionists to use the press as a weapon against slavery.

Around the turn of the present century a revolution in journalism made it possible for the reform journalist to communicate with a wide reading audience. A mass newspaper readership had been created by such enterprisers as Pulitzer and Hearst, who capitalized on the popular appeal of human interest stories. New techniques of printing and distribution led to cheaper popular magazines that attracted a readership previously unable to afford the élite periodicals. Circulation figures soared as genteel literature was replaced with articles that pricked America's social conscience.

A literature of exposure already existed during the later decades of the nineteenth century. Henry Adams exposed the corruption of the "Gilded Age" in his novel, *Democracy;* and in the '80's and '90's Henry Demarest Lloyd scrutinized the operations of John D. Rockefeller and the Standard Oil Company. In his *Wealth Against Commonwealth,* Lloyd revealed Rockefeller as a monopolist who employed unethical methods in pursuit of his business objectives. More generally, Lloyd argued that the rise of monopoly challenged American democracy and that the giant corporations should be socialized. But Lloyd was a gentleman radical whose writings were an extension of his personal involvement in social movements. In his day exposure was the work of isolated individuals.

During the years of the Roosevelt and Taft administrations, the first phase of the Progressive period, the literature of exposure attained a central position in the discussion of public affairs. Labelled "muckrakers" by Theodore Roosevelt, the crusading journalists of those years were professional writers who portrayed themselves as objective observers of society, reporting conditions as they found them. They were recruited by the popular magazines and assigned to topics suggesting dramatic stories of serious misconduct. The muckrakers mounted a comprehensive campaign of exposure and a number of writers established national reputations through their involvement in the movement. Hundreds of thousands read the articles of Lincoln Steffens, Ida Tarbell and Ray Stannard Baker and they became important molders of public opinion. Frequently, they advised the political reform leaders and, during Theodore Roosevelt's administration, had access to the White House. Muckraking also gave a new public status to the magazine publisher. Such men as Frank Munsey and especially S. S. McClure controlled magazines with great power to shape the public mind. With an intuitive genius McClure fused muckraking articles with new European and American fiction of high quality.

The muckrakers examined a wide variety of social problems, and few in public life were immune from the writers' searching criticism. In the business world the oil industry, life insurance and high finance took turns as the focus of muckraking interest. Ray Stannard Baker wrote of the race issue in the South and of the role of the labor movement. Steffens scrutinized the workings of urban corruption and went on to look at conditions on the state level. David Graham Phillips touched a raw nerve when he muckraked the American Senate and accused senators of treason for serving the corporations rather than the people. Trinity Church in New York was revealed as a slum landlord. Upton Sinclair dramatized the risk of consuming packing-house products. The various exposés added up to a verdict; the institutions that controlled the economic and political system were not to be trusted. The outer appearances of respectability concealed selfish interest and private profit took precedence over the public welfare.

In a speech in April, 1906, Theodore Roosevelt coined the term "muckraker" and warned against overstressing the negative aspects of American life. Roosevelt was concerned that the muckrakers might serve the purposes of the radicals, who sought a basic reconstruction of the social order. Soon afterwards the muckraking movement entered its period of decline and, by the middle of Woodrow Wilson's first term in the White House, was defunct.

Since the movement's demise, there have been periodic attempts to resurrect the muckraking technique as a necessary means of upholding the democratic tradition. Limited-circulation magazines of differing opinions represent some link with the older tradition. In such periods of social crisis as the Depression decade, muckraking has reappeared as a significant force. However, the modern reader has little acquaintance with muckraking literature. Lincoln Steffens is recalled for his *Autobiography*, particularly for his "Boy on Horseback." Upton Sinclair is known for his novels and because his career has stretched into our own period. But Ida Tarbell is hardly remembered at all, and Ray Stannard Baker only because his *Following the Color Line* is useful to students of the contemporary civil rights crisis.

Fortunately for those interested in renewing acquaintance with the muckrakers and their critique of society, there is a critical literature that attempts to set the crusaders in perspective. Beginning with the years of the Progressive Movement there has been controversy over the merits or defects of muckraking. Several of the muckrakers concerned themselves with evaluating their efforts. At the heart of the discussion has been the depth of the muckraker critique. Were the journalists crusaders, or sensationalists whose social analysis did not go beneath the surface? Is there anything of lasting value in the literary tradition set by the muckrakers? Did the muckrakers provide a major impetus of significant social change, or did they merely foster the illusion of effective action? Were the muckrakers in fact a vanguard of reform or mainly hired professionals who supplied what the public already wanted? Even the veracity of the various exposés has been questioned.

The selections included in this volume begin with Louis Filler's portrait of the typical muckraker. The muckraker in the various stages of his career reflected the values of the broader society. In Theodore Roosevelt's administration he threw himself into the work of reform and, when the war came, typically he agreed that Junkerism had to be crushed. The muckraker maintained his commitment to democracy and, even at the end of his career, he remained an optimistic progressive. This is not a full profile but rather an outline sketch of the muckraking temperament.

Following are four selections presenting various contemporary reactions to the movement. President Roosevelt recognizes the merit of exposure but warns against a negative approach he considers destructive. Roosevelt sought to restrain the drive that threatened to carry the country beyond reform into radicalism; he had been alarmed by David Graham Phillips' articles picturing important senators as corporation agents. Upton Sinclair argues the case for a positive appraisal of muckraking; as a Socialist he welcomed what he saw as the drift of the muckrakers toward an overtly anti-capitalist position. Dunne's Mr. Dooley offers another perspective: muckraking is a routine ritual of self-purification. There is public furor and moral excitement but actually the business system remains intact. Rounding out this group of selections is Walter Lippmann's evaluation. Lippmann sees the muckrakers as the product of their era who supplied what the readers desired. The public had good reason to be discontented with things as they were. New standards were set for the performance of the businessman and the corporation. The limitation of the muckrakers was their failure to explore the sources of this public expectation. For Lippmann muckraking was neither progressive nor reactionary.

Following the contemporary discussion of muckraking is a group of selections that focuses on the role of muckraking as literature. Robert Cantwell advances the view that muckraking represented a revolution in literature, a turning to themes of social reality, replacing an earlier literature of fantasy and polite manners. Ironically, the popular magazines for which the muckrakers wrote later became the vehicles of a mass popular literature devoid of controversy. Lewis Mumford's essay contends that the central defect of muckraking was its failure to examine the quality of American culture, its failure to confront the impoverishment of ethical and cultural values. Harvey Swados suggests that the literary works of the muckrakers were generally of poor quality but argues for the lasting value of the writers' journalistic efforts.

The next group of selections explores the influence of the muckraking movement on the reforms accomplished in the Progressive era. Parrington sees muckraking as the brilliant segment of a "comet of reform." In his view, the reformers continued the Enlightenment tradition of democratic reform. Their exposés provoked enormous disturbance and were a serious threat to the corporations. This explains why the campaign was brought to an end by business pressure on the magazines. Still, in Parrington's view, the more solid contribution to reform was made by such scholars as J. Allen Smith and Charles Beard, who struck at the intellectual defenses of the business system. C. C. Regier credits the muckraking movement with a considerable amount of influence on the impressive number of reforms accomplished between 1900 and 1915. Muckraking went out of fashion because some of the evils it had attacked were remedied and because to some extent it was merely a fad.

John Chamberlain's essay reflects the disillusionment of the 1930's radicals who found the muckraker approach inadequate. Chamberlain in 1932 censured the muckrakers for not seeing that collectivism was a necessary answer to the creed of economic individualism.

The final group of selections, arranged in two parts, contains several recent reappraisals of the muckraking era. The first part focuses on a muckraking classic, Lincoln Steffens' *Shame of the Cities*. The introduction to Steffens' book is presented, and following this two historians evaluate the adequacy of the muckraking view of urban politics and the accuracy of Steffens' indictment of urban corruption. Arthur Dudden finds Steffens' analysis to be essentially sound, but Samuel P. Hays, viewing a different city, raises some fundamental questions about Steffens' views concerning the problems of urban reform.

The second part raises questions about the muckrakers' social analysis. Louis Filler returns with some further thoughts about the muckrakers and compares their record favorably with that of later liberals. He underscores their contribution to reform while recognizing that they were not masters of theoretical abstraction. Richard Hofstadter finds a spirit of self-accusation in muckraking journalism and asserts that the primary role of the muckraker was to provide a catharsis for middle-class guilt. David Chalmers' essay appraises the muckrakers as constructive social critics who called attention to the changes that were transforming American society. Chalmers' analysis rejects the view that the muckrakers yearned for a return to a preindustrial order. Louis Geiger, however, argues that the muckrakers failed to develop a national synthesis of reform because of their inability to perceive the interlocking nature of urban and agrarian problems. The agrarian middle class never accepted the problems of the city as their own, nor did they feel any guilt for the sins of an urbanized society. The muckrakers' failure to create a truly national ideology of reform laid the groundwork for the separation between urban and rural progressivism that weakened the reform movement in the 1920's.

Whatever meaning Americans today give to democratic tradition, fulfillment of that heritage demands an informed public opinion. The problems now are more complex, but vigorous public debate and dissent are still among the best means of participation in the decision-making process of a democratic political system. The muckrackers addressed themselves to the task of social criticism that would arouse support for measures of reform. We can benefit from an understanding of their techniques and an appraisal of their success or failure as educators of the people of their generation.

CONTENTS

The Clash of Issues

An' there ye ar-re, Hinnissy. Th' noise ye hear is not th' first gun iv a rivolution. It's on'y th' people iv th' United States batin' a carpet.

FINLEY PETER DUNNE

Now, it is very necessary that we should not flinch from seeing what is vile and debasing. There is filth on the floor, and it must be scraped up with the muckrake. . . . But the man who never does anything else . . . speedily becomes, not a help to society, not an incitement to good, but one of the most potent forces of evil.

THEODORE ROOSEVELT

The substantial result of the movement was the instruction it afforded in the close kinship between business and politics — a lesson greatly needed by a people long fed on romantic unrealities.

VERNON LOUIS PARRINGTON

We come . . . to the conclusion that to a considerable extent muckraking was little more than a fad. Many writers took up muckraking because, for the time being, it was more profitable than other forms of writing. . . . Naturally they turned to other fields the moment it seemed likely that greater profit lay therein.

C. C. REGIER

The wielders of the muckrake exposed corruption in order that it might be corrected. Their analysis of national life probed deeply into the vast changes that had taken place during the previous half-century.

DAVID CHALMERS

Consider who the muckrakers were, what their intentions were, and what it was they were doing. Their criticisms of American sociey were, in their utmost reaches, very searching and radical, but they were themselves moderate men who intended to propose no radical remedies. From the beginning then, they were limited by the disparity between the boldness of their means and the tameness of their ends.

RICHARD HOFSTADTER

The ardent American notion of a free society, freely inclusive, freely elected, and freely helpful, had been cynically shoved aside in the closing decades of the nineteenth century. If it was revivified in the early years of the new century, to the benefit of every American who has come of age since then, that must be credited in substantial measure to the ringing voices of the muckrakers. . . .

HARVEY SWADOS

What the American worker needed in literature was discipline, confidence, heroic pictures, and large aims; what he got even from the writers who preached his emancipation was the notion that his distressing state was only the result of the capitalists' villainy and his own virtues. . . . For all the effect that these painstaking pictures had in lifting the worker onto a more active plane of manhood, one would willingly trade the whole literature for a handful of good songs.

LEWIS MUMFORD

I. A COMPOSITE PROFILE

Louis Filler: THE WAY OF A CRUSADING LIBERAL

Professor Louis Filler has written extensively concerning various social movements in American history. His Crusaders for American Liberalism *(1939) is a major full-length study of the muckrakers. In this introductory essay Professor Filler presents a profile of the typical muckraker.*

HE WAS born in the Eighteen Sixties, anywhere in the West — the Midwest, perhaps — where the pioneer had driven stakes and set about building a city. He was raised in the shadow of momentous events. In his boyhood he felt the tide of immigration rising about him, and watched the endless building of houses and breaking of new ground. Here he became conscious of large, rude enterprise, of industry, immeasurable and complex, always developing, restlessly on the move.

The boy was of good native stock, of intelligent and hardworking parents, who brought him up simply, on the old principles of plain living and high thinking, to respect his elders and do his work. He did his chores, played, read. He felt inspired by his early studies in American history and listened attentively to the tales of those who had served in the War. He accepted Lincoln naturally as the greatest of the latter-day gods.

He was soundly educated and, as he grew up, cherished literary ambitions. Being young and radical in his college days, he was thrilled by Mark Twain's work and thought it much more impor-

tant than his professors believed; Walt Whitman, on the other hand, was a strange experience, a perplexing problem in esthetics. Like most Western children he had been aware of politics almost as early as his cradle days, and now he learned to argue the tariff question and to discuss the greenback and anti-monopolist theories.

After college he faced the question of a career. He wanted to write literature but drifted inevitably into journalism, which was alive and offered more chances for work. So far as he could judge, the magazines were practically impenetrable. So he became a newspaperman and was sent about to report the news of the day. Enjoying a first-hand view of contemporary America, he was deeply impressed by the great factories and ships and railroads, the incoming droves of immigrants, the big city's slums, strikes, and wealth and poverty elbow to elbow. These things were far from literature, but they were life; they were real; and they destroyed forever his youthful desires for the Free Life— life after Murger and the Latin Quarter. This new America needed description

From Louis Filler, *Crusaders for American Liberalism* (New York, 1939). Reprinted by permission of the author.

and explanation, and perhaps even reform; it was a bad, splendid America; a serious, farcical, gaudy, unsophisticated America, seething with new thoughts and new problems.

Alert and intelligent, our journalist looked deeper than the ordinary man into these things, read widely to acquaint himself with modern political thought, tried to understand the forces working beneath the exterior of American life. Meanwhile he married, lived regularly, worked hard, found little time to squander. He attempted serious writing. He traveled in America mostly on business, and went to Europe to admire the emblems of age-old culture and maturity that were in evidence on every hand. The system and economy that he saw there he wished his own country, too, could show. Yet he loved home and was jealous for her. . . .

Our liberal was intensely nationalistic and individualistic, yet watching the steady growth of the corporations, the octopus-spread of railroad power, he tinkered with thoughts of government ownership and regulation. He could see labor's point of view, its need for unified action; he was sympathetic with the problems facing reformers. As for religion, his work and habits allowed him little time or inclination to carry on with the church as his fathers had done, and he thought of it chiefly with disapproval of its unprogressiveness, its tendency to cling to reaction. If the world of affairs was changing, he felt that the church, too, should be modernizing its ways.

With the rise of Theodore Roosevelt, the young journalist gave himself wholeheartedly to the new movement for exposure and reform. These great days kept him busy from morning to night. He bloomed; his powers were free and absolute. An eager public accorded him

a hearing, praise and honor, and money. He redoubled his efforts, writing the facts of contemporary life in the style that journalism had developed for him: a clear, bold, straightforward style, concerning itself with facts and figures. Only a few years ago "elegant" qualities had been prized in the literary man; our journalist-reformer sent them into the discard overnight.

He surveyed the "reconstructed" South, visited the factories and townships of New England, explored the far corners of the West and the Territories. He described the men and managements of the great industries and painted vivid pictures of the methods by which they operated. He reviewed the history of the country to find out how we had come to the age of trusts and corruptionists. He recounted with approval the efforts of the new social worker, the new reformer and statesman. And his articles made news that no one could resist reading.

The "muckraker," for so he soon came to be called, dealt with facts and not with theory. Whatever it was he concluded about business and the theory of capitalism—and he reached various conclusions—he made sure to give the facts and details about his subject. He described a lynching with realism, probed the psychology and history of the Rockefellers and Goulds, told intimate stories of the Tammany machine. Conservatives called him a sensationalist; critics and writers in the old tradition, whose stock had fallen low, accused him of being a mere journalist. In his "blue" moments, he was inclined to agree that he was a journalist; but then he would conclude that whether he was or was not, there had never before been such journalism as this.

II. THE MUCKRAKERS AND THEIR CONTEMPORARIES

Theodore Roosevelt: SPEECH, APRIL 14, 1906

The reform journalists were first described as "muckrakers" by Theodore Roosevelt in a speech delivered April 14, 1906. The occasion was the laying of a cornerstone of the new House of Representatives office building. Roosevelt recognized some value in the muckrakers' work, but he saw grave dangers that resulted from stressing the shortcomings of society. After reading the speech, Lincoln Steffens told the President, "Well, Mr. President, you have put an end to all these journalistic investigations that have made you."

OVER a century ago Washington laid the cornerstone of the Capitol in what was then little more than a tract of wooded wilderness here beside the Potomac. We now find it necessary to provide by great additional buildings for the business of the government. This growth in the need for the housing of the government is but a proof and example of the way in which the nation has grown and the sphere of action of the national government has grown. We now administer the affairs of a nation in which the extraordinary growth of population has been outstripped by the growth of wealth and the growth in complex interests. The material problems that face us today are not such as they were in Washington's time, but the underlying facts of human nature are the same now as they were then. Under altered external form we war with the same tendencies toward evil that were evident in Washington's time, and are helped by the same tendencies for good. It is about some of these that I wish to say a word today.

In Bunyan's *Pilgrim's Progress* you may recall the description of the Man with the Muckrake, the man who could look no way but downward, with a muckrake in his hands; who was offered a celestial crown for his muckrake, but who would neither look up nor regard the crown he was offered, but continued to rake to himself the filth of the floor.

In *Pilgrim's Progress* the Man with the Muckrake is set forth as the example of him whose vision is fixed on carnal instead of on spiritual things. Yet he also typifies the man who in this life consistently refuses to see aught that is lofty, and fixes his eyes with solemn intentness only on that which is vile and debasing. Now, it is very necessary that we should not flinch from seeing what is vile and debasing. There is filth on the floor, and it must be scraped up with the muckrake; and there are times and places where this service is the most needed of all the services that can be performed. But the man who never does anything else, who never thinks or speaks or writes save of his feats with the muckrake, speedily becomes, not a help to society, not an incitement to good, but one of the most potent forces of evil.

There are in the body politic, economic and social, many and grave evils, and there is urgent necessity for the sternest war upon them. There should be relentless exposure of and attack upon every evil man, whether politician or businessman, every evil practice, whether in politics, in business or in social life. I hail as a benefactor every writer or speaker, every man who, on the platform or in book, magazine or newspaper, with merciless severity makes such attack, provided always that he in his turn remembers that the attack is of use only if it is absolutely truthful. The liar is no whit better than the thief, and if his mendacity takes the form of slander he may be worse than most thieves. It puts a premium upon knavery untruthfully to attack an honest man, or even with hysterical exaggeration to assail a bad man with untruth. An epidemic of indiscriminate assault upon character does not good but very great harm. The soul of every scoundrel is gladdened whenever an honest man is assailed, or even when a scoundrel is untruthfully assailed.

Now, it is easy to twist out of shape what I have just said, easy to affect to misunderstand it, and, if it is slurred over in repetition, not difficult really to misunderstand it. Some persons are sincerely incapable of understanding that to denounce mudslinging does not mean the indorsement of whitewashing; and both the interested individuals who need whitewashing and those others who practice mudslinging like to encourage such confusion of ideas. One of the chief counts against those who make indiscriminate assault upon men in business or men in public life is that they invite a reaction which is sure to tell powerfully in favor of the unscrupulous scoun-

drel who really ought to be attacked, who ought to be exposed, who ought, if possible, to be put in the penitentiary. If Aristides is praised overmuch as just, people get tired of hearing it; and overcensure of the unjust finally and from similar reasons results in their favor.

Any excess is almost sure to invite a reaction; and, unfortunately, the reaction, instead of taking the form of punishment of those guilty of the excess, is very apt to take the form either of punishment of the unoffending or of giving immunity, and even strength, to offenders. The effort to make financial or political profit out of the destruction of character can only result in public calamity. Gross and reckless assaults on character —whether on the stump or in newspaper, magazine or book—create a morbid and vicious public sentiment, and at the same time act as a profound deterrent to able men of normal sensitiveness and tend to prevent them from entering the public service at any price. As an instance in point, I may mention that one serious difficulty encountered in getting the right type of men to dig the Panama Canal is the certainty that they will be exposed, both without, and, I am sorry to say, sometimes within, Congress, to utterly reckless assaults on their character and capacity.

At the risk of repetition let me say again that my plea is, not for immunity to, but for the most unsparing exposure of, the politician who betrays his trust, of the big businessman who makes or spends his fortune in illegitimate or corrupt ways. There should be a resolute effort to hunt every such man out of the position he has disgraced. Expose the crime and hunt down the criminal; but remember that even in the case of crime, if it is attacked in sensational, lurid and untruthful fashion, the attack may do more damage to the public mind than the crime itself. It is because I feel that there should be no rest in the endless war against the forces of evil that I ask that the war be conducted with sanity as well as with resolution. The men with the muckrakes are often indispensable to the well-being of society, but only if they know when to stop raking the muck, and to look upward to the celestial crown above them, to the crown of worthy endeavor. There are beautiful things above and round about them; and if they gradually grow to feel that the whole world is nothing but muck their power of usefulness is gone. If the whole picture is painted black there remains no hue whereby to single out the rascals for distinction from their fellows. Such painting finally induces a kind of moral color blindness; and people affected by it come to the conclusion that no man is really black and no man really white, but they are all gray. In other words, they neither believe in the truth of the attack nor in the honesty of the man who is attacked; they grow as suspicious of the accusation as of the offense; it becomes well-nigh hopeless to stir them either to wrath against wrongdoing or to enthusiasm for what is right; and such a mental attitude in the public gives hope to every knave, and is the despair of honest men.

To assail the great and admitted evils of our political and industrial life with such crude and sweeping generalizations as to include decent men in the general condemnation means the searing of the public conscience. There results a general attitude either of cynical belief in and indifference to public corruption or else of a distrustful inability to discriminate between the good and the bad. Either attitude is fraught with untold damage to the country as a whole. The fool who has not sense to discriminate between what is good and what is bad is well-nigh as dangerous as the man who does discriminate and yet chooses the bad. There is nothing more distressing to every good patriot, to every good American, than the hard, scoffing spirit which treats the allegation of dishonesty in a public man as a cause for laughter. Such laughter is worse than the crackling of thorns under a pot, for it denotes not merely the vacant mind, but the heart in which high emotions have been choked before they could grow to fruition.

There is any amount of good in the world, and there never was a time when loftier and more disinterested work for the betterment of mankind was being done than now. The forces that tend for evil are great and terrible, but the forces of truth and love and courage and honesty and generosity and sympathy are also stronger than ever before. It is a foolish and timid no less than a wicked thing to blink the fact that the forces of evil are strong, but it is even worse to fail to take into account the strength of the forces that tell for good. Hysterical sensationalism is the very poorest weapon wherewith to fight for lasting righteousness. The men who with stern sobriety and truth assail the many evils of our time, whether in the public press, or in magazines, or in books, are the leaders and allies of all engaged in the work for social and political betterment. But if they give good reason for distrust of what they say, if they chill the ardor of those who demand truth as a primary virtue, they thereby betray the good cause and play into the hands of the very men against whom they are nominally at war.

In his *Ecclesiastical Polity* that fine old Elizabethan divine, Bishop Hooker, wrote:

"He that goeth about to persuade a multitude that they are not so well governed as they ought to be, shall never want attentive and favorable hearers; because they know the manifold defects whereunto every kind of regimen is subject, but the secret lets and difficulties, which in public proceedings are innumerable and inevitable, they have not ordinarily the judgment to consider."

This truth should be kept constantly in mind by every free people desiring to preserve the sanity and poise indispensable to the permanent success of self-government. Yet, on the other hand, it is vital not to permit this spirit of sanity and self-command to degenerate into mere mental stagnation. Bad though a state of hysterical excitement is, and evil though the results are which come from the violent oscillations such excitement invariably produces, yet a sodden acquiescence in evil is even worse. At this moment we are passing through a period of great unrest—social, political and industrial unrest. It is of the utmost importance for our future that this should prove to be not the unrest of mere rebelliousness against life, of mere dissatisfaction with the inevitable inequality of conditions, but the unrest of a resolute and eager ambition to secure the betterment of the individual and the nation. So far as this movement of agitation throughout the country takes the form of a fierce discontent with evil, of a determination to punish the authors of evil, whether in industry or politics, the feeling is to be heartily welcomed as a sign of healthy life.

If, on the other hand, it turns into a mere crusade of appetite against appetite, of a contest between the brutal greed of the "have-nots" and the brutal greed of the "haves," then it has no significance for good, but only for evil. If it seeks to establish a line of cleavage, not along the line which divides good men from bad, but along that other line, running at right angles thereto, which divides those who are well off from those who are less well off, then it will be fraught with immeasurable harm to the body politic.

We can no more and no less afford to condone evil in the man of capital than evil in the man of no capital. The wealthy man who exults because there is a failure of justice in the effort to bring some trust magnate to an account for his misdeeds is as bad as, and no worse than, the so-called labor leader who clamorously strives to excite a foul class feeling on behalf of some other labor leader who is implicated in murder. One attitude is as bad as the other, and no worse; in each case the accused is entitled to exact justice; and in neither case is there need of action by others which can be construed into an expression of sympathy for crime.

It is a prime necessity that if the present unrest is to result in permanent good the emotion shall be translated into action, and that the action shall be marked by honesty, sanity and self-restraint. There is mighty little good in a mere spasm of reform. The reform that counts is that which comes through steady, continuous growth; violent emotionalism leads to exhaustion.

It is important to this people to grapple with the problems connected with the amassing of enormous fortunes, and the use of those fortunes, both corporate and individual, in business. We should discriminate in the sharpest way between fortunes well won and fortunes ill won; between those gained as an incident to performing great services to the community as a whole, and those gained in evil fashion by keeping just within the limits of mere law-honesty. Of course no amount of charity in spending such fortunes in any way compensates for misconduct in making them. As a matter of personal conviction, and without pretending to discuss the details or formulate the system, I feel that we shall ultimately have to consider the adoption of some such scheme as that of a progressive tax on all fortunes, beyond a certain amount, either given in life or devised or bequeathed upon death to any individual—a tax so framed as to put it out of the power of the owner of one of these enormous fortunes to hand on more than a certain amount to any one individual; the tax, of course, to be imposed by the national and not the state government. Such taxation should, of course, be aimed merely at the inheritance or transmission in their entirety of those fortunes swollen beyond all healthy limits.

Again, the national government must in some form exercise supervision over corporations engaged in interstate business—and all large corporations are engaged in interstate business—whether by license or otherwise, so as to permit us to deal with the far-reaching evils of overcapitalization. This year we are making a beginning in the direction of serious effort to settle some of these economic problems by the railway rate legislation. Such legislation, if so framed, as I am sure it will be, as to secure definite and tangible results, will amount to something of itself; and it will amount to a great deal more in so far as it is taken as a first step in the direction of a policy of superintendence and control over corporate wealth engaged in interstate commerce, this superintendence and control not to be exercised in a spirit of malevolence toward the men who have created the wealth, but with the first purpose both to do justice to them and to see that they in their turn do justice to the public at large.

The first requisite in the public servants who are to deal in this shape with corporations, whether as legislators or as executives, is honesty. This honesty can be no respecter of persons. There can be no such thing as unilateral honesty. The danger is not really from corrupt corporations; it springs from the corruption itself, whether exercised for or against corporations.

The eighth commandment reads, "Thou shalt not steal." It does not read, "Thou shalt not steal from the rich man." It does not read, "Thou shalt not steal from the poor man." It reads simply and plainly, "Thou shalt not steal." No good whatever will come from that warped and mock morality which denounces the misdeeds of men of wealth and forgets the misdeeds practiced at their expense; which denounces bribery, but blinds itself to blackmail; which foams with rage if a corporation secures favors by improper methods, but merely leers with hideous mirth if the corporation is itself wronged. The only public servant who can be trusted honestly to protect the rights of the public against the misdeed of a corporation is that public man who will just as surely protect the corporation itself from wrongful aggression. If a public man is willing to yield to popular clamor and do wrong to the men of wealth or to rich corporations, it may be set down as certain that if the opportunity comes he will secretly and furtively do wrong to the public in the interest of a corporation.

But, in addition to honesty, we need sanity. No honesty will make a public man useful if that man is timid or foolish, if he is a hot-headed zealot or an impracticable visionary. As we strive for reform we find that it is not at all merely the case of a long uphill pull. On the contrary, there is almost as much of breeching work as of collar work; to depend only on traces means that there will soon be a runaway and an upset. The men of wealth who today are trying to prevent the regulation and control of their business in the interest of the public by the proper government authorities will not succeed, in my judgment, in checking the progress of the movement. But if they did succeed they would find that they had sown the wind and would surely reap the whirlwind, for they ultimately provoke the violent excesses which accompany a reform coming by convulsion instead of by steady and natural growth.

On the other hand, the wild preachers of unrest and discontent, the wild agitators against the entire existing order, the men who act crookedly, whether because of sinister design or mere puzzle-headedness, the men who preach destruction without proposing any substitute for what they intend to destroy, or who propose a substitute which would be far worse than the existing evils—all these men are the most dangerous opponents of real reform. If they get their way they will lead the people into a deeper pit than any into which they could fall under the present system. If they fail to get their way they will still do incalculable harm by provoking the kind of reaction which in its revolt against the senseless evil of their teaching would enthrone more securely than ever the very evils which their misguided followers believe they are attacking.

More important than aught else is the development of the broadest sympathy of man for man. The welfare of the wage worker, the welfare of the tiller of the soil, upon these depend the welfare of the entire country; their good is not to be sought in pulling down others; but their good must be the prime object of all our statesmanship.

Materially, we must strive to secure a broader economic opportunity for all men, so that each shall have a better chance to show the stuff of which he is made. Spiritually and ethically we must strive to bring about clean living and right thinking. We appreciate that the things of the body are important; but we appreciate also that the things of the soul are immeasurably more important. The foundation stone of national life is, and ever must be, the high individual character of the average citizen.

Finley Peter Dunne: NATIONAL HOUSECLEANING

> *Finley Peter Dunne was one of the outstanding figures of American journalism around the turn of the century. His specialty was a biting satirical wit expressed in the sayings of a fictional Irish-American, Mr. Dooley. In the article "National Housecleaning" (1906) the humorist presents his view of the muckraking movement.*

From Finley Peter Dunne, *Dissertations by Mr. Dooley* (Harper & Row, Publishers, Inc., 1906), pp. 257–262.

"IT LOOKS to me," said Mr. Hennessy, "as though this counthry was goin' to th' divvle."

"Put down that magazine," said Mr. Dooley. "Now d'ye feel betther? I thought so. But I can sympathize with ye. I've been readin' thim mesilf. Time was whin I sildom throubled thim. I wanted me fiction th' day it didn't happen, an' I cud buy that f'r a penny fr'm h' newsboy on th' corner. But wanst in a while some homefarin' wandhrer wud jettison wan in me place, an' I'd frequently glance through it an' find it in me lap whin I woke up. Th' magazines in thim days was very ca'ming to th' mind. Angabel an' Alfonso dashin' f'r a marredge license. Prom'nent lady authoressses makin' pomes at th' moon. Now an' thin a scrap over whether Shakespeare was enthered in his own name or was a ringer, with th' long-shot players always again Shakespeare. But no wan hurt. Th' idee ye got fr'm these here publications was that life was wan glad, sweet song. If annything, ivrybody was too good to ivrybody else. Ye don't need to lock th' dure at night. Hang ye'er watch on th' knob. Why do polismen carry clubs? Answer, to knock th' roses off th' throlley-poles. They were good readin'. I like thim th' way I like a bottle v white pop now an' thin.

"But now whin I pick me fav'rite magazine off th' flure, what do I find? Ivrything has gone wrong. Th' wurruld is little betther thin a convict's camp. Angabel an' Alfonso ar-re about to get marrid whin it is discovered that she has a husband in Ioway an' he has a wife in Wisconsin. All th' pomes be th' lady authoressses that used to begin: 'Oh, moon, how fair!' now begin: 'Oh, Ogden Armour, how awful!' Shakespeare's on'y mintioned as a crook. Here ye ar-re. Last edition. Just out. Full account iv th'

Crimes iv Incalculated. Did ye read Larsen last month on 'Th' use iv Burglars as Burglar Alarums'? Good, was it? Thin read th' horrible disclosures about th' way Jawn C. Higgins got th' right to build a bay-window on his barber-shop at iliven forty-two Kosciusko Avnoo, South Bennington, Arkansaw. Read Wash'n'ton Bliffens's dhreadful assault on th' board iv education iv Baraboo. Read Idarem on Jawn D.; she's a lady, but she's got th' punch. Graft ivrywhere. 'Graft in th' Insurance Comp'nies,' 'Graft in Congress,' 'Graft in th' Supreem Coort,' 'Graft be an Old Grafter,' 'Graft in Lithrachoor,' be Hinnery James; 'Graft in Its Relations to th' Higher Life,' be Dock Eliot; 'Th' Homeeric Legend an' Graft; Its Cause an' Effect; Are They th' Same? Yes and No,' be Norman Slapgood.

"An' so it goes, Hinnissy, till I'm that blue, discouraged, an' broken-hearted I cud go to th' edge iv th' wurruld an' jump off. It's a wicked, wicked, horrible, place, an' this here counthry is about th' toughest spot in it. Is there an honest man among us? If there is throw him out. He's a spy. Is there an institution that isn't corrupt to its very foundations? Don't ye believe it. It on'y looks that way because our graft iditor hasn't got there on his rounds yet. Why, if Canada iver wants to increase her popylation all she has to do is to sind a man in a balloon over th' United States to yell: 'Stop thief!' At th' sound iv th' wurruds sivinty million men, women, an' little scoundhrelly childher wud skedaddle f'r th' frontier, an' lave Jerome, Folk, an' Bob La Follette to pull down th' blinds, close th' dure, an' hang out a sign: 'United States to rent.' I don't thrust anny man anny more. I niver did much, but now if I hear th' stealthy step iv me dearest frind at th' dure I lock th' cash dhrawer. I used to be nervous about burglars, but now I'm afraid iv a night call fr'm th' Chief Justice iv th' Supreem Coort or th' prisidint iv th' First National Bank.

"It's slowly killin' me, Hinnissy, or it wud if I thought about it. I'm sorry George Wash'n'ton iver lived. Thomas Jefferson I hate. An' as f'r Adam, well, if that joker iver come into this place I'd —but I mustn't go on.

"Do I think it's all as bad as that? Well, Hinnissy, now that ye ask me, an' seein' that Chris'mas is comin' on, I've got to tell ye that this counthry, while wan iv th' worst in th' wurruld, is about as good as th' next if it ain't a shade betther. But we're wan iv th' gr-reatest people in th' wurruld to clean house, an' th' way we like best to clean th' house is to burn it down. We come home at night an' find that th' dure has been left open an' a few mosquitoes or life-insurance prisidints have got in, an' we say: 'This is turr'ble. We must get rid iv these here pests.' An' we take an axe to thim. We desthroy a lot iv furniture an' kill th' canary bird, th' cat, th' cuckoo clock, an' a lot iv other harmless insects, but we'll fin'lly land th' mosquitoes. If an Englishman found mosquitoes in his house he'd first thry to kill thim, an' whin he didn't succeed he'd say: 'What pleasant little humming-bur-rds they ar-re. Life wud be very lonesome without thim,' an he'd domesticate thim, larn thim to sing 'Gawd Save th' King,' an' call his house Mosquito Lodge. If these here inthrestin' life-insurance scandals had come up in Merry ol' England we'd niver hear iv thim, because all th' boys wud be in th' House iv Lords be this time, an' Lord Tontine wud sit hard on anny scheme to have him searched be a lawyer fr'm Brooklyn. But with this here nation iv ours somebody scents something wrong with th' scales at th' grocery-store an' whips out his gun, another man turns in a fire alarm, a third fellow sets fire to th' Presbyterian Church, a vigilance comity is formed an' hangs ivry foorth man; an' havin' started with Rockyfellar, who's tough an' don't mind bein' lynched, they fin'lly wind up with desthroyin' me because th' steam laundhry has sint me home somebody else's collars.

"It reminds me, Hinnissy, iv th' time I lived at a boardin'-house kept be a lady be th' name iv Doherty. She was a good woman, but her idee iv life was a combination iv pneumony an' love. She was niver still. Th' sight iv a spot on th' wall where a gintleman boorder had laid his head afther dinner would give her nervous prostration. She was always polishin', scrubbin', sweepin', airin'. She had a plumber in to look at th' dhrains twice a week. Fifty-two times a year there was a rivolution in th' house that wud've made th' Czar iv Rooshya want to go home to rest. An' yet th' house was niver really clean. It looked as if it was to us. It was so clean that I always was ashamed to go into it onless I'd shaved. But Mrs. Doherty said no; it was like a pig-pen. 'I don't know what to do,' says she. 'I'm worn out, an' it seems impossible to keep this house clean.' 'What is th' throuble with it?' says he. 'Madam,' says me frind Gallagher 'wud ye have me tell ye?' he says. 'I wud,' says she. 'Well,' says he, 'th' throuble with this house is that it is occypied entirely be human bein's,' he says. 'If 'twas a vacant house,' he says, 'it cud aisily be kept clean,' he says.

"An' there ye ar-re, Hinnissy. Th' noise ye hear is not th' first gun iv a rivolution It's on'y th' people iv th' United State batin' a carpet. Ye object to th' smell That's nawthin'. We use sthrong disin fectants here. A Frinchman or an En glishman cleans house be sprinklin' th' walls with cologne; we chop a hole in th' flure an' pour in a kag iv chloride iv lime. Both are good ways. It depinds on how long ye intind to live in th' house. What were those shots? That's th' house-keeper killin' a couple iv cockroaches with a Hotchkiss gun. Who is that yellin'? That's our ol' friend High Finance bein' compelled to take his annual bath. Th' housecleanin' season is in full swing, an' there's a good deal iv dust in th' air; but I want to say to thim neighbors iv ours, who're peekin' in an' makin' remarks about th' amount iv rubbish, that over in our part iv th' wurruld we don't sweep things undher th' sofa. Let thim put that in their pipes an' smoke it."

"I think th' counthry is going to th' divvle," said Mr. Hinnissy, sadly.

"Hinnissy," said Mr. Dooley, "if that's so I congratylate th' wurruld."

"How's that?" asked Mr. Hennessy.

"Well," said Mr. Dooley, "f'r nearly forty years I've seen this counthry goin' to th' divvle, an' I got aboord late. An' if it's been goin' that long an' at that rate, an' has got no nearer thin it is this pleasant Chris'mas, thin th' divvle is a divvle iv a ways further off thin I feared."

Upton Sinclair: THE MUCKRAKE MAN

With his novel The Jungle, *which vividly described conditions in the Chicago meat-packing industry, Upton Sinclair emerged as one of the significant figures of the Progressive era. Sinclair saw socialism as the solution to the problems of modern capitalism, and the following essay is a defense of the muckraking movement from the standpoint of the radical.*

ALL proper-minded people are agreed that the Muckrake Man is a noxious weed; yet he seems to flourish persistently. He is a hardy plant, difficult to keep down and impossible to destroy. Apparently he possesses within him some strange conviction which enables him to withstand obloquy.

It should occur to the thoughtful person that this powerful impulse to make oneself disagreeable must be worth inquiring about. What is it which gives to this unpleasant weed its extraordinary vitality?

In setting down my interpretation of the phenomenon, I am not speaking for myself personally; I know, more or less intimately, nearly every man who is at present raking muck in America, and I believe that I am able to speak from the standpoint of the group.

The Muckrake Man takes himself with tremendous seriousness. He believes that he serves a vital function in society: that he is no less than the faculty of recollection in the growing social mind. He is the particular nerve cell in the burned child which cries out to the child, Do

From Upton Sinclair, "The Muckrake Man," *The Independent* (September, 1908), pp. 517–519).

not put your finger into the fire again!
He represents the effort of the race to
profit by experience, and to do otherwise
than repeat indefinitely the blunders
which have proved fatal in the past.

If you will stop for a moment and consider, you will realize that the history of
humanity up to the present time represents a series of failures. Races emerge
from barbarism. They are joyous and
proud and strong; they struggle and con-
quer, they toil and achieve. They build
mighty cities and temples; they found
courts of law; they write literatures and
produce arts. But all the time there is a
worm within the bud, which gnaws at it;
and just when the flower seems most
perfect, its petals fall, and it is scattered
and trampled into the dust.

Now, to the earnest student who real-
izes this, it seems a very pitiful thing.
Civilizations are such costly affairs. It
seems too bad that no way can be found
to save them. Here and there is a man
to whom this thought becomes an obses-
sion—it will not let him rest.

He sees a beautiful world about him,
with stars and flowers and all sorts of
things that interest him. He knows of
many things he would like to do and to
be, many ways in which he could amuse
himself. And yet, instead of this, he be-
gins to go about pointing out disagreeable truths to people. He says: "See, we
are just like Rome. Our legislatures are
corrupt; our politicians are unprincipled;
our rich men are ambitious and unscrupulous. Our newspapers have been purchased and gagged; our colleges have
been bribed; our churches have been
cowed. Our masses are sinking into degradation and misery; our ruling classes
are becoming wanton and cynical."

This has been said in our country for
a generation. Abraham Lincoln said it,
for one. All earnest students knew it. But

the public merely laughed incredulously.

And then comes the Muckrake Man.
He says to himself, "This is a serious
matter. It cannot be neglected. The
people will not believe it—but I will
prove it to them!"

And so he proceeds to gather the
evidence.

This is a very easy part of the Muckrake Man's task—realizing how easy it is,
one might wonder why the trade is not
more frequently followed. The Muckrake Man suffers only from the embar-
rassment of riches. His greatest labor is
in rejecting. In whatever field he may
elect to work, he finds one universal
maxim prevailing: "Everybody knows."
He finds that it is sometimes possible to
get the actors themselves to confess to
him. Frequently they will tell him the
facts without even realizing their significance. "Why, my dear fellow," said a
Chicago packer to me, when I confronted
him with certain matters which con-
vulsed two continents—"everybody knows
these things. They are conventions of
the trade. See, here, they are printed in
catalogs"—and he proceeded to show me
the prices of materials for adulterating
and preserving spoiled meat.

Again, I talked with a young lawyer
who had been prominent in one of the
big life insurance companies. "My dear
fellow," he said, "there was nothing
wrong in the life insurance business. It
was just that the public lost its head.
We have been doing those things all our
lives, and we are doing them still."

Again, I talked with a judge of the
Supreme Court of New York about another judge who had paid $25,000 for his
nomination. "My dear fellow," he said,
"don't you suppose that a political machine has bills to pay?"

Again, I talked with a society woman,
whose name is a household word in this

country. "My dear fellow," she said, "those things are so obvious. Why do you want to put them into a book? People will simply call it a rehash." I answered: "I will put what you have told me into a book, and it will be received with a howl of incredulity from Maine to California."

This being the situation, it would seem that the Muckrake Man would have an easy time of it; it would seem that he should speedily win the friendship of the public, in whose behalf he works. But, unfortunately, the public takes its opinions from the newspapers; and the newspapers are owned by men who profit by corruption. Hence it is that the Muckrake Man and his work are regarded with aversion.

You will observe that the one thing that is never done to him is to refute his statements. You very seldom hear of any attempt to disprove the statements of the Muckrake Man. I know one who for six or eight years has been publishing facts about corruption in our cities and States; and in all that time he has never been corrected but twice. Once he published an acknowledgment of a misstatement; and in the other case he said to me, "I was foolish to publish that. It is true, but it is incredible. That is where you fall down, Sinclair. You refuse to eliminate the incredible."

No, the editorial authority never refutes the facts; he sits aloft in his editorial sanctum and scorns to know anything about facts. Instead, he calls names.

He says, in the first place, that the Muckrake Man has an evil imagination; he has a nose for corruption, he thrives upon scandal, he hates humanity. Now the Muckrake Men I know are all men of personally clean lives and generous hearts; there is not one of them who would not have been something noble, if he had felt free to choose. Of those who come immediately to my mind, one would have been a metaphysician, another would have been a professor of ethics, three at least would have been poets, and one would have founded a new religion. Instead of that they are Muckrake Men. But they are Muckrake Men, not because they love corruption, but simply because they hate it with an intensity which forbids them to think about anything else while corruption sits enthroned.

Next, the editorial authority charges that the Muckrake Man is a money-seeker; that he gathers up other people's misdeeds and turns them into cash for his own benefit. Now, the Muckrake Man is one of the hardest-working men I know. He does not work eight hours a day, and then rest; he works all the time that he is awake—and his work has a tendency to keep him awake. He is always a man of exceptional brain power; and if, instead of writing indictments of rich corruptionists, he were writing briefs to defend them, he would be earning a hundred thousand a year, and would be a welcome guest upon steam yachts and private trains. As it is, he generally lives alone in a couple of rooms in a quiet hotel, labors for several months over an article, and then sells it for a few hundred dollars.

Next, we are told by the editorial authority that the Muckrake Man is a notoriety-hunter. Of course, if he had leagued himself with the corrupting class, and had played the game according to their rules, he might have hunted all the notoriety he chose. He might have become a magnate, and endowed libraries and charitable institutions, and been known as a great philanthropist. He might have purchased a leading newspaper, and had himself made an Ambassador, and been a guest of kings. He might have become a leading college president, or a bishop, or some other maker of public opinion, and been wined at Civic Federation banquets and hailed by all the newspapers of the country as a natural born leader. Instead of that, he goes by himself, and writes the truth relentlessly, and publishes it with grief and despair in his soul; and he is called a notoriety-hunter.

As a rule, the Muckrake Man began his career with no theories, as a simple observer of facts known to every person at all "on the inside" of business and politics. But he followed the facts, and the facts always led him to one conclusion; until finally he discovered to his consternation that he was enlisted in a revolt against capitalism.

He is the forerunner of a revolution; and, like every revolutionist, he takes his chances of victory and defeat. If it is defeat that comes; if the iron heel wins out in the end—why, then, the Muckrake Man will remain for all time a scandal-monger and an assassin of character. If, on the other hand, he succeeds in his efforts to make the people believe what "everybody knows"—then he will be recognized in future as a benefactor of his race.

Walter Lippmann: THE THEMES OF MUCKRAKING

For more than half a century Walter Lippmann has been a foremost commentator on American society and world affairs. In his book Drift and Mastery *(1914) he sought to analyze the changes in American life that gave impetus to the Progressive movement. His first chapter, "The Themes of Muckraking," represents an early attempt to set muckraking in perspective. Muckraking evoked a remarkable response from the reading public, and Lippmann offers an explanation of that response.*

THERE is in America to-day a distinct prejudice in favor of those who make the accusations. Thus if you announced that John D. Rockefeller was going to vote the Republican ticket it would be regarded at once as a triumph for the Democrats. Something has happened to our notions of success: no political party these days enjoys publishing the names of its campaign contributors, if those names belong to the pillars of society. The mere statement that George W. Perkins is an active Progressive has put the whole party somewhat on the defensive. And there is more than sarcasm in the statement of the *New York Times Annalist* that:

"If it be true that the less bankers have to do with a scheme of banking and currency reform the more acceptable

From Walter Lippmann, *Drift and Mastery: An Attempt to Diagnose the Current Unrest* (New York, Mitchell Kennerley, 1914), pp. 1–26.

it will be to the people, it follows that the Administration's Currency Bill . . . must command popular admiration."

You have only to write an article about some piece of corruption in order to find yourself the target of innumerable correspondents, urging you to publish their wrongs. The sense of conspiracy and secret scheming which transpire is almost uncanny. "Big Business," and its ruthless tentacles, have become the material for the feverish fantasy of illiterate thousands thrown out of kilter by the rack and strain of modern life. It is possible to work yourself into a state where the world seems a conspiracy and your daily going is beset with an alert and tingling sense of labyrinthine evil. Everything askew—all the frictions of life are readily ascribed to a deliberate evil intelligence, and men like Morgan and Rockefeller take on attributes of omnipotence, that ten minutes of cold sanity would reduce to a barbarous myth. I know a socialist who seriously believes that the study of eugenics is a Wall Street scheme for sterilizing working-class leaders. And the cartoons which pictured Morgan sitting arrogantly in a chariot drawn by the American people in a harness of ticker tape—these are not so much caricatures as pictures of what no end of fairly sane people believe. Not once but twenty times have I been told confidentially of a nation-wide scheme by financiers to suppress every radical and progressive periodical. But even though the most intelligent muckrakers have always insisted that the picture was absurd, it remains to this day a very widespread belief. I remember how often Lincoln Steffens used to deplore the frightened literalness with which some of his articles were taken. One day in the country he and I were walking the railroad track. The ties, of course, are not well spaced for an ordinary stride, and I complained about it. "You see," said Mr. Steffens with mock obviousness, "Morgan controls the New Haven and he prefers to make the people ride."

Now it is not very illuminating to say that this smear of suspicion has been worked up by the muckrakers. If business and politics really served American need, you could never induce people to believe so many accusations against them. It is said, also, that the muckrakers played for circulation, as if that proved their insincerity. But the mere fact that muckraking was what people wanted to hear is in many ways the most important revelation of the whole campaign.

There is no other way of explaining the quick approval which the muckrakers won. They weren't voices crying in a wilderness, or lonely prophets who were stoned. They demanded a hearing; it was granted. They asked for belief; they were believed. They cried that something should be done and there was every appearance of action. There must have been real causes for dissatisfaction, or the land notorious for its worship of success would not have turned so savagely upon those who had achieved it. A happy husband will endure almost anything, but an unhappy one is capable of flying into a rage if his carpet-slippers are not in the right place. For America, the willingness to believe the worst was a strange development in the face of its traditional optimism, a sign perhaps that the honeymoon was over. For muckraking flared up at about the time when land was no longer freely available and large scale industry had begun to throw vast questions across the horizon. It came when success had ceased to be easily possible for everyone.

The muckrakers spoke to a public willing to recognize as corrupt an incredibly varied assortment of conventional acts. That is why there is nothing mysterious or romantic about the business of exposure—no putting on of false hair, breaking into letter-files at midnight, hypnotizing financiers, or listening at keyholes. The stories of graft, written and unwritten, are literally innumerable. Often muckraking consists merely in dressing up a public document with rhetoric and pictures, translating a court record into journalese, or writing the complaints of a minority stockholder, a dislodged politician, or a boss gone "soft." No journalist need suffer from a want of material.

Now in writing this chapter I started out to visualize this material in systematic and scholarly fashion by making a list of the graft revelations in the last ten years. I wished for some quantitative sense of the number and kinds of act that are called corrupt. But I found myself trying to classify the industrial, financial, political, foreign and social relations of the United States, with hundreds of sub-heads, and a thousand gradations of credibility and exaggeration. It was an impossible task. The popular press of America is enormous, and for years it has been filled with "probes" and "amazing revelations." And how is a person to classify, say, the impeachment of a Tammany governor by a Tammany legislature? A mere list of investigations would fill this book, and I abandoned the attempt with the mental reservation that if anyone really desired that kind of proof, a few German scholars, young and in perfect health, should be imported to furnish it.

They could draw up a picture to stagger even a jaded American. Suppose they began their encyclopedia with the adulteration of foods. There would follow a neat little volume on the aliases of coffee. The story of meat would help the vegetarians till the volume on canned foods appeared. Milk would curdle the blood, bread and butter would raise a scandal, candy—the volume would have to be suppressed. If photographs could convey odors the study of restaurant might be done without words. The account of patent medicines, quack doctors, beauty parlors, mining schemes, loan sharks, shyster lawyers, all this riff raff and fraud in the cesspool of commercialism would make unendurable reading. You would rush to the window cursing the German pedants, grateful for a breath of that air which filters through in spite of the unenforced smoke ordinance of your city.

But the story would proceed. Think of your state of mind after you had read all about the methods of drummers, advertising agents, lobbyists, publicity men after you knew adulteration of every description, and had learned the actual motives and history of political conferences, of caucuses, and consultations with the boss; suppose you understood the underground history of legislatures, the miscarriages of justice, the relations of the police to vice and crime, of newspapers to advertisers and wealthy citizens, of trade union leaders to their unions, the whole fetid story of the war between manufacturers and labor organizations. A study of the public domain in America would employ a staff of investigators. What railroads have done to the public, to their employees, what directors do to the stockholders and the property, the quantitative record of broken trust, the relation of bankers to the prosperity of business enterprise, of stock gamblers to capitalization—taking merely all that is known and could be illustrated, summed up and seen at once, what a picture it would make.

And yet such a picture would be false and inept. For certainly there must be some ground for this sudden outburst of candor, some ground beside a national desire for abstract truth and righteousness. These charges and counter-charges arose because the world has been altered radically, not because Americans fell in love with honesty. If we condemn what we once honored, if we brand as criminal the conventional acts of twenty years ago, it's because we have developed new necessities and new expectations.

They are the clue to the clouds of accusation which hang over American life. You cannot go very far by reiterating that public officials are corrupt, that business men break the law. The unbribed official and the law-abiding business man are not ideals that will hold the imagination very long. And that is why the earlier kind of muckraking exhausted itself. There came a time when the search for not-dishonest men ceased to be interesting. We all know now what tepid failures were those first opponents of corruption, the men whose only claim to distinction was that they had done no legal wrong. For without a vivid sense of what politics and business might be, you cannot wage a very fruitful campaign.

Now if you study the chief themes of muckraking I think it is possible to see the outlines of what America has come to expect.

The first wave of exposure insisted upon the dishonesty of politicians. Close upon it came widespread attack upon big business men, who were charged with bribing officials and ruining their competitors. Soon another theme appeared: big business men were accused of grafting upon the big corporations which they controlled. We are entering upon another period now: not alone big business, but all business and farming too, are being criticized for inefficiency, for poor product, and for exploitation of employees.

This classification is, of course, a very rough one. It would be easy enough to dispute it, for the details are endlessly complicated and the exceptions may appear very large to some people. But I think, nevertheless, that this classification does no essential violence to the facts. It doesn't matter for my purposes that some communities are still in what I call the first period, while others are in the third. For a nation like ours doesn't advance at the same rate everywhere. All I mean to suggest is that popular muckraking in the last decade has shifted its interest in something like this order: First, to the corruption of aldermen and mayors and public servants by the boss acting for a commercial interest, and to the business methods of those who built up the trusts. Then, muckraking turned, and began to talk about the milking of railroads by banks, and of one corporation by another. This period laid great emphasis on the "interlocking directorate." Now, muckraking is fastening upon the waste in management, upon working conditions as in the Steel Mills or at Lawrence, or upon the quality of service rendered by the larger corporations. These have been the big themes.

Why should they have been? Why, to begin with, should politicians have been attacked so fiercely? Some people would say flatly: because politicians were dishonest. Yet that is an utterly unfounded generalization. The morals of politicians cannot by any stretch of the imagination be described as exceptionally bad. Politicians were on the make. To be sure. But who in this sunny land isn't? They gave their relatives and friends pleasant positions. What father doesn't do that for his son if he can, and with every feeling of righteousness? They helped their friends, they were loyal to those who had helped them: who will say that in private life these are not admirable virtues? And what were the typical grafts in politics—the grafts for which we tried to send politicians to jail? The city contracts for work, and the public official is in league with the contractor; but railroads also contract for work, and corporation officials are at least as frequently as politicians, financially interested in the wrong side of the deal. The city buys real estate, and the city official manages to buy it from himself or his friends. But railroad directors have been known to sell their property to the road they govern.

We can see, I think, what people meant by the word graft. They did not mean robbery. It is rather confused rhetoric to call a grafter a thief. His crime is not that he filches money from the safe but that he betrays a trust. The grafter is a man whose loyalty is divided and whose motives are mixed. A lawyer who takes a fee from both sides in some case; a public official who serves a private interest; a railroad director who is also a director in the supply company; a policeman in league with outlawed vice: those are the relationships which the American people denounce as "corrupt." The attempt to serve at the same time two antagonistic interests is what constitutes "corruption."

The crime is serious in proportion to the degree of loyalty that we expect. A President of the United States who showed himself too friendly to some private interest would be denounced, though he may not have made one cent out of the friendship. But where we have not yet come to expect much loyalty we do very little muckraking. So if you inquired into the ethics of the buyer

in almost any manufacturing house, you would find him doing things daily that would land the purchasing agent of a city in jail. Who regards it as especially corrupt if the selling firm "treats" the buyer, gives him or her a "present," perhaps a commission, or at least a "good time"? American life is saturated with the very relationship which in politics we call corrupt. The demand for a rake-off . . . saturates the work-a-day world with tips and fees and "putting you on to a good thing" and "letting you in on the ground floor." But in the politician it is mercilessly condemned.

That is because we expect more of the politician. We say in effect that no public servant must allow himself to follow the economic habits of his countrymen. The corrupt politician is he who brings into public service the traditions of a private career. Perhaps that is a cynical reflection. I do not know how to alter it. When I hear politicians talk "reform," I know they are advocating something which most drummers on the road would regard as the scruples of a prig, and I know that when business men in a smoking-room are frank, they are taking for granted acts which in a politician we should call criminal.

For the average American will condemn in an alderman what in his partner he would consider reason for opening a bottle of champagne. In literal truth the politician is attacked for displaying the morality of his constituents. You might if you didn't understand the current revolution, consider that hypocrisy. It isn't: it is one of the hopeful signs of the age. For it means that unconsciously men regard some of the interests of life as too important for the intrusion of commercial ethics.

Run a government to-day, with the same motives and vision that you run a dry goods store, and watch for the activ ty of the muckrakers. Pursue in the post office the methods which made you a ounder of colleges, you will be grateful or a kind word from Mr. Lorimer. Poor is they are, the standards of public life ire so much more social than those of business that financiers who enter polics regard themselves as philanthropists. The amount of work and worry without eward is almost beyond the comprehension of the man whose every act is meaured in profit and loss. The money to be accumulated in politics even by the ynically corrupt is so small by comparion that able men on the make go into politics only when their motives are mixed with ambition, a touch of idealsm, vanity, or an imaginative notion of uccess.

But the fact that a public official took no bribe soon ceased to shield him from popular attack. Between the honest adierent of machine politics and the coruptionist himself the muckrakers made to sharp distinction. And that was beause they had in a vague way come to xpect positive action from men in office. They looked for better school systems, or health campaigns, or a conservation policy, that is for fairly concrete social measures, and officials who weren't for hem were lumped together and deounced. The official might have read too much Adam Smith, or been too much of a lawyer, or taken orders from the boss, or a bribe from a lobbyist—the ough result was the same: he wasn't for what public opinion had come to expect, and the muckrakers laid their traps for him.

I suppose that from the beginning of he republic people had always expected heir officials to work at a level less selfeeking than that of ordinary life. So hat corruption in politics could never be carried on with an entirely good concience. But at the opening of this century, democratic people had begun to see much greater possibilities in the government than ever before. They looked to it as a protector from economic tyranny and as the dispenser of the prime institutions of democratic life.

But when they went to the government, what they found was a petty and partisan, slavish and blind, clumsy and rusty instrument for their expectations. That added to the violence of their attacks. When they had no vision of what a democratic state might do, it didn't make so very much difference if officials took a rake-off. The cost of corruption was only a little money, and perhaps the official's immortal soul. But when men's vision of government enlarged, then the cost of corruption and inefficiency rose: for they meant a blighting of the whole possibility of the state. There has always been corruption in American politics, but it didn't worry people very much, so long as the sphere of government was narrowly limited. Corruption became a real problem when reform through state action began to take hold of men's thought.

As muckraking developed, it began to apply the standards of public life to certain parts of the business world. Naturally the so-called public service corporation was the first to feel the pressure. There is obviously a great difference in outlook between the Vanderbilt policy of "the public be damned" and the McAdoo policy of "the public be pleased." The old sense of private property is very much modified: few railroad men to-day would deny that they are conducting a quasi-public enterprise, and that something more is demanded of them than private exploitation. Thus President Mellen of the New Haven railroad could not have been handled more roughly by the people of New England if they had elected him to office. And his successor,

President Howard Elliott, finds it necessary to remind the people that "the railroad is a public servant in fact as well as in name and that the service which it renders depends largely upon the treatment which it receives from its master." Mr. Elliott's grandfather would, I think, have said that his descendant lacked a sense of private property. That is true: Mr. Elliott's remark is a recognition that the cultural basis of property is radically altered, however much the law may lag behind in recognizing the change. So if the stockholders think they are the ultimate owners of the Pennsylvania railroad, they are colossally mistaken. Whatever the law may be, the people have no such notion. And the men who are connected with these essential properties cannot escape the fact that they are expected to act increasingly as public officials.

That expectation has filtered into the larger industrial corporations. I have here, for example, a statement by Roger Babson, a recognized financial expert:

"Suppose the mayor of a town should appoint his brother police commissioner; his daughter's husband, fire commissioner; his uncle, superintendent of the water works; and put his son in charge of the street cleaning department. How long would it be before the good citizens would hold an indignation meeting? It would not be long. No city in America would stand that kind of graft. Yet pick up the letterhead of a private corporation and what are you likely to find? It usually reads something like this: Quincy Persimmon, president; Quincy Persimmon, Jr., vice-president; Persimmon Quincy, treasurer; Howard Lemon, secretary. The presence of Howard Lemon in this select family circle is somewhat puzzling until one learns that Prunella Quincy Persimmon is the wife of Howard Lemon. Then all is clear. . . ."

Now when the Persimmons are muckraked, what puzzles them beyond words is that anyone should presume to meddle with *their* business. What they will learn is that it is no longer altogether *their* business. The law may not have realized this, but the fact is being accomplished and it's a fact grounded deeper than statutes. Big business men who are at all intelligent recognize this. They are talking more and more about their "responsibilities," their "stewardship." It is the swan-song of the old commercial profiteering and a dim recognition that the motives in business are undergoing a revolution. . . .

Why all this has happened: why there are new standards for business men, why the nature of property is altered, why the workers and the purchasers are making new demands—all this muckraking never made very clear. It was itself considerably more of an effect than a sign of leadership. It expressed a change, and consequently it is impossible to say that muckraking was either progressive or reactionary in its tendency. The attack upon business men was listened to by their defeated competitors as well as by those who looked forward to some better order of industrial life. Muckraking is full of the voices of the beaten, of the bewildered, and then again it is shot through with some fine anticipation. It has pointed to a revolution in business motives; it has hinted at the emerging power of labor and the consumer—we can take those suggestions, perhaps, and by analyzing them, and following them through, gather for ourselves some sense of what moves beneath the troubled surface of events.

III. MUCKRAKING AS LITERATURE

Robert Cantwell: JOURNALISM — THE MAGAZINES

Robert Cantwell, novelist and critic, evaluates the muckraking magazines as "making an original contribution to American literature and to American social life." Stress is placed on the special qualities that gave the muckrakers a wide reading audience.

EARLY in May, 1906, an extraordinary group of journalists walked out of the most sensationally successful magazine in American history. They left in a body. There were two men from the business department, an associate editor, the managing editor and his assistant, and three of the most celebrated magazine writers of the time—Ida Tarbell, Lincoln Steffens, and Ray Stannard Baker. Ida Tarbell was nearly fifty; she had written her lives of Lincoln and her famous *History of the Standard Oil Company.* Steffens was celebrating his fortieth birthday at the time of the walkout; he had published his *Shame of the Cities* and had been in Colorado, working on an article on Ben Lindsay, when the break came. Baker had not at that time written his best sellers under the name of David Grayson, but he was widely known, and he had been with the magazine through the six years of its greatest growth. These writers were joined by William Allen White and Finley Peter Dunne; they raised $200,000, bought *The American Magazine* and set out to rival the magazine they had left.

This was *McClure's.* Founded thirteen years before by the ambitious, volatile Samuel Sidney McClure, it had swept into an exhilarating financial, political, and literary success so rapidly that no other publication of its time could be compared to it. When it was founded, American periodical publishing was dominated by the four great, venerable, distinguished literary magazines—*Harpers, Scribners,* the *Atlantic* and *Century.* Modelled on the English magazines, printing genteel fiction by some highly skilled practitioners and a good deal of expertly composed but unexciting literary criticism, they had never been really popular. *Harpers* led them with a circulation of 130,000. This was, however, as great a circulation as any American magazine had up to that time, with the brief exception of *Godey's Lady's Book,* which had reached 150,000 in 1850. Indeed, it was commonly believed then that Americans were not magazine readers, just as it is generally believed now that they will not buy books: Poe had increased the circulation of *Gresham's* from 6000 to 30,000, but Henry Adams, despite some distinguished contributors and some timely

Extract from "Journalism — The Magazines" by Robert Cantwell is reprinted with the permission of Charles Scribner's Sons from *America Now,* edited by Harold E. Stearns, pp. 345–349. Copyright 1938 Charles Scribner's Sons; renewal copyright © 1966 Elizabeth Chalifoux Chapin.

articles, could not get *The North Ameri-can Review* above 2000. That had been the tradition when McClure and Munsey launched their cheap magazines. By the time Steffens and Tarbell left in 1906, popular magazines were firmly estab-lished in American cultural life: *Mc-Clure's* alone had a circulation of 750,000. More importantly, a group of magazines with similar policies had swept up with it: *Hampton's* increased from 13,000 to 440,000; *Everybody's*, which had been the house organ for Wanamaker's de-partment store, climbed to 735,000; *Collier's* had 500,000 by 1909 and one million by 1912; *Cosmopolitan* and *The American Magazine* grew in proportion. Consequently, when Steffens and Tarbell left *McClure's* it was no mere editorial squabble—American popular magazines, and not simply *McClure's* and the muck-rakers, had come into existence during their careers. Largely, in fact, as a result of their bold and simultaneous editorial coups—*The History of the Standard Oil Company* and *The Shame of the Cities*. When they began these works there were no popular American magazines; when they left *McClure's*, magazines had something of the popularity, and a good deal of the character, that they have now.

The term muckrakers applied to these people is as misleading now as it was when Ellery Sedgwick, then a young journalist, first tagged them with it — for it was Sedgwick and not Roosevelt who first applied Bunyan's phrase to describe them. Why had they been so sensation-ally successful? The commonly accepted answer has been that their exposures of the corruption of American political and social life coincided with a great stirring of popular revolt. Theirs was, Parrington says, "a dramatic discovery . . . when the corruption of American politics was laid on the threshold of business — like a bas-tard on the doorstep of the father — a tremendous disturbance resulted. There was a great fluttering and clamor amongst the bats and the owls. . . ." The political side of the muckrakers' contri-bution was unquestionably great, but it has been overvalued, and the simple journalistic boldness and effectiveness of their writing has been overlooked. After thirty years the simple bulk of their work is astonishing; in five years' time a hand-ful of gifted writers conducted a search-ing exploration of American society— industrial, financial, political, and moral. Moreover, they did this with a wealth of local color, with wonderful savory names and places that had never been elevated into prose before. It was not because the muckrakers exposed the corruption of Minneapolis, for example, that they were widely read, but because they wrote about Minneapolis at a time when it had not been written about, without patron-izing or boosting it, and with an attempt to explore its life realistically and intelligently.

They wrote, in short, an intimate anecdotal, behind-the-scenes history of their own times — or, rather, they tried to write it, for they often fell down. They traced the intricate relationship of the police, the underworld, the local political bosses, the secret connections between the new corporations (then consolidat-ing at an unprecedented rate) and the legislatures and the courts. In doing this they drew a new cast of characters for the drama of American society: bosses professional politicians, reformers, racke-teers, captains of industry. Everybody recognized these native types; everybody knew about them; but they had not been characterized before; their social func-tions had not been analyzed. At the same time, the muckrakers pictured stage set ings that everybody recognized but that nobody had written about — oil refineries, slums, the redlight districts, the hotel rooms where political deals were made — the familiar, unadorned, homely stages where the teeming day-to-day dramas of American life were enacted. How could the aloof literary magazines of the East, with their essays and their contributions from distinguished English novelists, tap this rich material?

For literary, and not for political reasons, the muckrakers were successful. Their writing was jagged and hasty, and their moralizing now sounds not only dull but a little phony, yet they charged into situations that were deliberately obscured by the people involved in them; they sized up hundreds of complicated and intense struggles at their moment of greatest intensity; they dealt with material subject to great pressure and about which journalists could easily be misled. In a time of oppressive literary gentility they covered the histories of the great fortunes and the histories of corporations — something that had not been done before and that has scarcely been done well since — the real estate holdings of churches, the ownership of houses of prostitution, insurance scandals, railway scandals, the political set-ups of Ohio, Missouri, Wisconsin, Chicago, Cleveland, San Francisco, New York. The new huge cities of the West had not been explored after their growth through the 70's and 80's (just as, say, Tulsa, Oklahoma, has not been written about after its astonishing growth through the 920's) and because they wrote of them, the writing of the muckrakers was packed with local color, the names and appearance of hotels and bars, crusading ministers and town bosses and bankers. They told people who owned the factories they worked in, who rigged the votes they cast, who profited from the new bond issue, the new street-railway franchise and the new city hall, who foreclosed the mortgage, tightened credit, and controlled the Irish vote on the other side of the river. Their exposures, as such, were not so sensational. People knew all the scandals, and worse ones. But they liked to read about towns they knew, characters they recognized, and a setting they understood. The old magazines had never given them that.

American popular magazines thus began by making an original contribution to American literature and to American social life. . . . [They] began by distributing a literature of information and inquiry — even of discontent — a kind of writing, which, for all its unevenness, was calculated to inform readers of the life of communities like their own, and to stimulate skeptical discussion of their institutions. Having gained circulation in this way, they insensibly shifted and began to distribute a different kind of reading matter which has grown into the magazine literature we now have. It would be wrong to imply that the owners and advertisers were solely responsible for this; the limitations of the muckrakers, their inability to set any new goal for themselves once their initial survey was completed, was as great a factor. In any event a literature that was, in a studied way, not political and not controversial came into being and became the chief product of the popular magazines.

Lewis Mumford: THE SHADOW OF THE MUCKRAKE

Lewis Mumford is an outstanding critic of modern American culture and the process of urbanization. In his book The Golden Day (*1926*) *he focuses on aspects of American cultural history. A chapter, "The Shadow of the Muck-Rake," is devoted to a literary evaluation of the muckraking effort.*

WITH the passing of the frontier in 1890, one special source of American experience dried up: the swell which between 1860 and 1890 had reached the Pacific Coast and had cast ashore its flotsam in a Mark Twain, a Bret Harte, a Muir, now retreated: the land-adventure was over. As a result, the interest in the industrial process itself intensified: the Edisons and Carnegies came to take the place in the popular imagination once occupied by Davy Crockett and Buffalo Bill. In books written for children there is a certain cultural lag which records the change of the previous generation very faithfully. The earliest children's books of the Nineteenth Century were moral tracts; they recorded the moment of Puritanism. The dime novel came in in the sixties, to echo the earliest exploits of the bad man and the outlaw; this was supplemented in the seventies by the books of Horatio Alger, written purely in the ideology of the Eighteenth Century, preaching self-help, thrift, success. In the late nineties a new set of children's books dealt with the frontiers and the Indian fights of the previous generation, to be supplanted, finally, by stories in which mechanical experiment and exploit predominated. Here is a brief revelation of our dominant idols.

With the concentration on machine industry went a similar concentration in finance. The eighties and nineties were the decades of great improvements in the steel industry, in stockyards, and in the applications of electricity; they also witnessed the first rude experiments with the internal combustion engine, which paved the way for the automobile and the aeroplane. Unfortunately, finance did not lag behind technology; and the directors of finance found methods of disposing of the unearned increment derived from land, scientific knowledge, social organization, and the common technological processes, for the benefit of the absentee owner rather than for the common welfare of the community.

The note of the period was consolidation. The great captains of industry controlled the fabrication of profits with a military discipline: they waged campaigns against their competitors which needed only the actual instruments of warfare to equal that art in ruthlessness; they erected palisades around their works; they employed private condottieri to police their establishments; they planted spies among their workers; and they viewed, doubtless with satisfaction, the building of armories in the big cities where the State Militia could be housed in time of stress to preserve "law and order." Herbert Spencer looked to industry

From *The Golden Day*, by Lewis Mumford, pp. 233–46. Dover Publications, Inc., New York, 1967. Reprinted through the permission of the author and of the publisher.

ry to supplant militarism; he had not reckoned that industry itself might be militarized, any more than he had seen that warfare might eventually be mechanized; but between 1890 and 1920 all these things came to pass. The workers themselves, after various efforts to achieve solidarity in a Socialist Party or in the Knights of Labor, met the challenge by adopting a pecuniary strategy: but unlike their financial antagonists, the captains of the American Federation of Labor permitted themselves to be handicapped by jurisdictional disputes and factional jealousies; and important new industries, like oil and steel, languished without even their modicum of financial protection.

What happened in industry happened likewise in all the instrumentalities of the intellectual life. This same period witnessed the vast mechanical accretion of Columbia University and Harvard, and the establishment of Leland Stanford (railroads) and the University of Chicago (oil). Stanley Hall recorded in his autobiography, with a noble restraint, the sort of ruthlessness with which President Harper of Chicago made away with the corps of instructors and professors all had gathered together at Clark University: Mr. Rockefeller never got hold of oil wells and pipe lines with more adroit piracy. The concentration of publishing houses and magazines in New York was a natural accompaniment of the financial process.

This consolidation and concentration completed in industry what the Civil War had begun in politics. The result was a pretty complete regimentation of our American cities and regions. While the process was fostered in the name of efficiency, the name refers only to the financial returns, and not to the industrial or social method. Without doubt

large efficiencies were achieved in the manufacture of monopoly profits, through special privilege, corporate consolidation, and national advertising; but the apologists for this regime were driven to express all these triumphs in the sole terms in which they were intelligible — money. In spite of its wholesale concentration upon invention and manufacture, in spite of its sacrifice of every other species of activity to utilitarian enterprise, this society did not even fulfill its own boast: it did not produce a sufficient quantity of material goods. Judged purely by its own standards, industrialism had fallen short. The one economist who devoted himself to explaining this curious failure, Mr. Thorstein Veblen, was dismissed as a mere satirist, because he showed that the actual economies of machine industry were forfeited to pecuniary aggrandizement, and through a wry standard of consumption — which confused wealth with pecuniary respectability and human vitality with keeping up appearances. For the controllers of industry, financial imperialism produced considerable profits; for the large part of the population it resulted in a bare subsistence, made psychologically tolerable by meretricious luxuries, once the sole property of a higher pecuniary caste. The Pittsburgh Survey ably documented current industrialism in every civic aspect; but it merely set down in cold print actualities which were open to any one who would take the trouble to translate bank accounts and annual incomes into their concrete equivalents.

It is no special cause for grief or wonder that the Army Intelligence tests finally rated the product of these depleted rural regions or of this standardized education, this standardized factory regime, this standardized daily routine as below the human norm in intelligence: the wonder would rather have been if any large part of the population had achieved a full human development. The pioneer, at worst, had only been a savage; but the new American had fallen a whole abyss below this: he was becoming an automaton. Well might Mark Twain ask in despair, What Is Man? "I have seen the granite face of Hawthorne," exclaimed Henry James, Senior, "and feel what the new race may be!" In less than two generations that feeling for a new human strength and dignity had been wiped out. The popular hero of the time was that caricature of humanity, a he-man, shrill, vituperative, platitudinous, equivocating. In art, the memorable figures, the human ones, were caricatures: Mr. Dooley, Potash and Perlmutter, Weber and Fields. They alone had a shape, a flavor.

The chief imaginative expression of this period came from men who were caught in the maw of the Middle West; and who, whatever their background, had been fed with the spectacle of this callow yet finished civilization, the last word in mechanical contrivance, scarcely the first faint babble in culture — sentimental yet brutal, sweet but savage. F. P. Dunne, George Ade, Ed Howe, Hamlin Garland, Theodore Dreiser, Edgar Lee Masters, Frank Norris, Robert Herrick — these were the writers who caught and expressed the spirit of this interregnum; and nearly all of these men had sprung out of the Middle West, or had had at least a temporary resting place in Chicago during their formative years. Jack London and Upton Sinclair belonged to this group in spirit, if not in locality. These writers departed from the complacency of the Gilded Age, if not from its pragmatic bias; they challenged the esoteric culture that attempted to snuggle on the ancient bosom of Europe in the name of a coarse but upstanding vigor derived completely from the life around them. Born between the close of the Civil War and 1880, by the place of their birth they had inherited the memories of the pioneer, by the time of their birth, those of industrialism and the new immigrant. Mawkish middle-class writers, like Meredith Nicholson and Booth Tarkington, saw this life through the genuine lace curtains of respectable parlors: but the more virile representatives of this period knew it from the saloon to the stockyard, from the darkest corner of the cellar to the top of the new skyscrapers.

II

The shadow of the muck-rake fell over this period. That was to its credit. But business went on as usual and the muck remained. Those who defended the sweating of labor, the building of slums, the bribery of legislatures, the piratical conduct of finance, the disorderly and short-sighted heaping up of very evanescent material goods were inclined to blame the muck-rake for the existence of the muck, just as they would blame the existence of labor agitators for the troubles they attempt to combat — which is very much like blaming the physician for the plague. As a result of the muck-rake, whitewash cans and deodorizing solutions came into general use: philanthropic bequests became more numerous and more socialized; social work expanded from the soup kitchens and down-and-out shelters to social settlements; and the more progressive factories even began to equip themselves with gymnasiums, lunchrooms, orchestras, and permanent nurses. If modern industrial society had in fact been in the blissful state its proponents always claimed, it would be hard indeed to account for all these remedial organizations; but in the widening of the concept of "charity" the claims of the critics, from Owen to Marx, were steadily being recognized.

Frank Norris, in *The Octopus* and *The Pit*, Upton Sinclair in *The Jungle*, and Jack London in the numerous biographic projections he called novels, faced the brutal industrialism of the period: they documented its workings in the wheatfield, the prison, the stockyard, the stock exchange, and the vast purlieus of *la ville tentaculaire;* Mr. Robert Herrick, a little more restrained but just as keenly awakened, added to the picture. The work that these men accomplished could scarcely be called a spiritual catharsis; nor it left the reader the same man that it found him; it was rather a regurgitation. To their credit, they confronted the life about them: they neither fled to Europe nor fancied that all American aspects were smiling ones. But these vast cities and vacant countrysides were not something that they took in and assimilated and worked over into a new pattern: it did not, in fact, occur to these writers that the imagination had an important part to play in the process. They were reporters, or, if they thought of themselves more pretentiously, social scientists; their novels were photographs, or at any rate campaign documents.

With unflinching honesty, these novelists dug into the more putrid parts of modern American society and brought to light corruption, debasement, bribery, greed, and foul aims. Fight corruption! Combat greed! Reform the system! Their conclusions, implicit or expressed, could all be put in some terse admonition. They took these symptoms of a deep social maladjustment to be the disease itself; they sought to reach them by prayer and exhortation, carried on by

street corner evangelists, by legislative action — or, if necessary, by a revolutionary uprising in the fashion of 1789.

Perhaps the most typical writers of this period were implicated in political programs for reform and revolution. In their reaction against the vast welter of undirected forces about them, they sought to pave the way for political changes which would alter the balance of political power, drive out the "predatory interests," and extend to industry itself the republican system of government in which the nation had been conceived. Upton Sinclair's *The Industrial Republic,* which followed close on his great journalistic beat, *The Jungle* — the smell of tainted meat, which accompanied the United States Army to Cuba, still hung in the air — was typical of what was good and what was inadequate in these programs. To Mr. Sinclair, as to Edward Bellamy some twenty years earlier, the Social Commonwealth, full-panoplied, was just behind the horizon. He was hazardous enough to predict its arrival within a decade. With Mr. Sinclair's aim to establish a more rational industrial order, in which function would supplant privilege, in which trained intelligence would take the place of inheritance, in which the welfare of the whole community would be the prime end of every economic activity, I am in hearty sympathy. What was weak in Mr. Sinclair's program was the assumption that modern industrial society possessed all the materials essential to a good social order. On this assumption, all that was necessary was a change in power and control: the Social Commonwealth would simply diffuse and extend all the existing values. These writers accepted the trust, and wanted the principle of monopoly extended: they accepted the bloated city, and wanted its subways and tenements socialized, as well as its waterworks; there were even authoritarian socialists, like Daniel De Leon, who believed that the corporate organization of workers, instead of being given added responsibility as guilds, would disappear entirely from the scene with the Socialist State. Concealed under revolutionary phrases, these critics could envisage only a bourgeois order of society, in which every one would have the comforts and conveniences of the middle classes, without the suffering, toil, anxiety, and frustration known to the unskilled worker.

What was lacking in such views was a concrete image of perfection: the "scientific" socialists distrusted utopias, and so made a utopia of the existing order. In attack, in criticism, they did able work; but when it came to offering a genuine alternative, their picture became a negative one: industry without millionaires, cities without graft, art without luxury, love without sordid calculation. They were ready to upset every aspect of modern industrial society except the fragmentary culture which had brought it into existence.

Now, were the diffusion of existing values all that was required of a better social order, the answer of capitalism was canny and logical: the existing regime could diffuse values, too. Did not bank accounts spread — and Ford cars — and movies — and higher wages in the skilled trades? What more could one want? Why risk one's neck for a Social Commonwealth when, as long as privilege was given a free hand, it would eventually provide the same things? Thus the socialist acceptance of the current order as a "necessary stage," and the socialist criticism, "Capitalism does not go far enough" have been answered by the proposition that it actually does go farther: the poor do not on the whole get poorer, but slowly march upward in the social scale.

The evils of privilege and irresponsible power in America were of course real; but the essential poverty of America was a qualitative poverty, one which cut through the divisions of rich and poor; and it has been this sort of poverty which has prevented us from projecting in the imagination a more excellent society. Life was more complicated in America but not more significant; life was richer in material goods but not in creative energies. These eager and relentless journalists were unaware of the necessity for establishing different kind of goods than the existing ones; they had no notion of other values, other modes other forms of activity than those practiced by the society around them. The result is that their works did not tend to lead out of the muddle. Their novel were interesting as social history; bu they did not have any formative effect for they sentimentalized the worker t the extent of always treating him as victim, and never making out of him hero. The only attempt to create a heroic portrait of the worker came towards th end of the muck-raking period; it wa that of Beaut McGregor in Sherwoo Anderson's *Marching Men*, a hal wrought figure in an imperfect book.

What the American worker needed i literature was discipline, confidenc heroic pictures, and large aims: what h got even from the writers who preache his emancipation was the notion that h distressing state was only the result the capitalist's villainy and his own vi tues, that the mysterious external force of social evolution were bound event ally to lift him out of his mean and su servient condition and therefore he ne not specially prepare himself to bri about this outcome — and that anyw he odds were always against him! It is doubtful whether this analysis could be called accurate science; it certainly was not high literature. For all the effect that these painstaking pictures had in lifting the worker into a more active plane of manhood, one would willingly trade the whole literature for a handful of good songs. I am not sure but that the rowdy, impoverished lyrics of the wobblies were not more stirring and formative — and that they may last longer, too.

Harvey Swados: YEARS OF CONSCIENCE

Harvey Swados is a well known novelist and social critic. In Years of Conscience (*1962*) *he presents a collection of muckraker writings. An introductory essay presents the view that the muckrakers made a substantial contribution to the democratic tradition. Swados gives his reasons for taking issue in part with Lewis Mumford's appraisal of muckraking.*

SOMETHING exhilarating happened to American journalism at the beginning of the twentieth century. For a brief period, a decade — roughly from 1902 to 1912 — an extraordinarily keen group of editors and publishers made common cause with some of the nation's outstanding novelists, poets, historians, lawyers, economists, and researchers. The cause, which changed the course of our history, was the exposure of the underside of American capitalism.

Ever since the Civil War there had been plenty of editors and writers willing and eager to inculcate a credulous public with legends of wealth accumulated solely by thrift and canniness, of progress achieved thanks to completely unregulated free enterprise, and of the natural inferiority of the lower orders: Ambrose Bierce argued against the socialists that slums and child labor ought not to be combated because they were the inevita-ble lot of those too stupid and shiftless to raise themselves and their offspring from the heap. But a new wind blew in with the new century, reintroducing two qualities which had for too long been relegated to the wings of the American scene: honesty and compassion.

Honesty was now defined not merely as "discretion" or "balance" but as unflinching determination to bring to light the reality behind the convenient myths about the rulers of America, regardless of whether the rulers' power lay in the political machine, in the corporate cannibalism tagged as the trust, or even in the pulpit. Compassion was now defined not merely as "charity" or "sympathy" but as outraged identification with the friendless and the voiceless at the bottom of society, regardless of whether they were illiterate croppers, sweated newcomers, aggrieved laborers, or terrorized Negroes.

From Harvey Swados, *Years of Conscience* (New York, 1962). Reprinted by permission of The World Publishing Company.

During this vigorous decade honesty in pushing the investigation of corporate and governmental corruption to its nethermost reaches and in arriving at the ultimate logical conclusions was not mislabeled treason, subversion, *lèse-majesté,* or cynicism. Nor was compassion for the suffering of the exploited millions — as ruthlessly sacrified in the rage to industrialize as the masses of any contemporary Communist ex-colony — mistaken for sentimentality, or confounded with the "square."

In fact, it was the Square Deal's father who also fathered the name which has identified these journalists from that day to this. On April 14, 1906, in the midst of the labors of this unusual band, Theodore Roosevelt unloosed an attack on them, taking as his text a passage from *Pilgrim's Progress:* ". . . the Man with the Muckrake, the man who could look no way but downward, with a muckrake in his hands; who was offered a celestial crown for his muckrake, but who would neither look up nor regard the crown he was offered, but continued to rake to himself the filth of the floor."

The presidential attack, sanctimonious and largely unjustified though it was, created a permanent label, one which has entered the language as has the more recent "egghead"; but it did not succeed in slowing the momentum of muckraking journalism. That did not take place until the end of the Taft administration, when B. H. Hampton, last of the great muckraking publishers, awoke one day in 1911 to find that financial control of *Hampton's,* a haven for writers displaced from other journals, had been maneuvered out of his hands and that the magazine was going to be scuttled — apparently by underground agreement of some of the financial interests which had been plagued by its revelations.

Historians differ as to whether muckraking was bought out and killed off, or whether — regardless of what happened to *Hampton's* — it would in any case have died with the ebbing of the Roosevelt era. Certainly some of the muckrakers themselves, tired, disillusioned, or disoriented by American participation in World War I, directed their energies into other channels; one became a corporation executive, another a chronicler of romances, a third a biographer, a fourth a professional reactionary.

But just as certainly, during the first decade of this century, these writers showed themselves at their best; and they, together with the editors and publishers who were bold and idealistic enough to commission and to print their exposes, showed America at its periodic best. There is something to be said for the notion that our country recuperates from its greedy decades almost like a repentant drunkard recovering from a debauch by trying to examine the causes of his drinking bout and by making earnest resolutions to sin no more. The difference between the nation and the drunkard may lie in the fact that in its moods of sober self-criticism the nation really does redress many of the wrongs really does help those who cannot help themselves, and does thereby renew its world image as a state concerned not solely, or even primarily, with self-aggrandizement, but much more importantly with dignity, freedom, and decent self-respect.

This is not to say that the national mood during these intervals of thoughtful stock-taking is always one of unalloyed benevolence, any more than were the pages of the muckraking magazines purely rationalistic or invariably redolent of Christian brotherhood. Just as the New Deal years were also the years of the Silver Shirts, the Liberty

League, and the German-American Bund, so can one find in the pages of the muckraking magazines reams of non-sensical food-faddism and, worse, occasional articles about semibarbaric Negroes or aggressively acquisitive Hebrews which should have been beneath the contempt of any self-respecting editor; and it is perfectly true that a humane, passionately reform-minded editor like B. O. Flower could wax as eloquent in the pages of *The Arena* over the virtues of spiritualism or Christian Science as over those of civic reform or public ownership. But we speak here of an overall tone, a mood, and it is surely beyond dispute that in those years such periodicals as *Hampton's*, *Pearson's*, the *Cosmopolitan*, and *McClure's*, to say nothing of *Collier's* or *The Arena*, reflected in their major concerns everything that has been traditionally largest and noblest in the American spirit.

That may very well explain the twofold reaction to Theodore Roosevelt's epithet on the part of the journalists whom he attacked. If Gustavus Myers and Ida Tarbell were appalled at this parodying of their scholarly researches, others — Upton Sinclair and Charles Edward Russell among them — responded to the challenge by accepting the label and insisting on wearing it with pride, as a proof of the force with which their work was striking home.

History would seem to justify those who gloried in TR's diatribe; for, decades later, the surviving journalists of the era vied in asserting pride of rank in the muckraking elite and in reading others out of it. This was to be true even of those (a majority of the original group) whose political philosophy had shifted over the years: Mark Sullivan, become a spokesman for conservative Republicanism, was to insist in his later years that he and not Lincoln Steffens

had fired the opening gun of the muckrakers' crusade. One hardly presses his claim to charter membership in a group which he cannot regard as representative of what is best in the national character.

It should not be thought that the muckrakers sprang full-blown from the brows of a handful of editors, any more than that their spirit was swept from the scene once and for all by the storm clouds of the First World War. Their fervor, their passionate denunciation of corporate aggrandizement at the expense of the individual American, their belief in the boundless possibilities of a better nation, instinct in every line they wrote — all these are to be found in Henry Demarest Lloyd's *Wealth Against Commonwealth*, which was published in 1894.

"The men and women who do the work of the world," asserted Lloyd in his opening chapter,

have the right to the floor. Everywhere they are rising to "a point of information." They want to know how our labor and the gifts of nature are being ordered by those whom our ideals and consent have made Captains of Industry over us; how it is that we, who profess the religion of the Golden Rule and the political economy of service for service, come to divide our partial existence for the many who are the fountains of these powers and pleasures. This book is an attempt to help the people answer these questions. It has been quarried out of official records, and it is a venture in realism in the world of realities. Decisions of courts and of special tribunals like the Interstate Commerce Commission, verdicts of juries in civil and criminal cases, reports of committees of the State Legislatures and of Congress, oathsworn testimony given in legal proceedings and in official inquiries, corrected by rebutting testimony and by cross-examination — such are the sources of information.

Indeed the only thing wrong with this powerful book, from a journalistic standpoint at least, was that it was too far in advance of its time, for it anticipated in every area the main lines of attack of the muckrakers; to a modern reader its method and its commitment are all but indistinguishable from those of the muckrakers, and if it was less widely absorbed than their work this can only be attributed to the fact that the public was "not ready" for it — which may be another way of saying that it was not made readily available as an article of mass consumption.

A decade later, however, the public was ready. Or again we may put this another way by saying that the revelations of the muckrakers were made easily available to the public by a mass medium, the cheap popular magazine. If it is worth noting that the traditional American periodicals — whether scholarly, historical, literary, or simply upper-class in general — played little part in the tumultuous activity of the decade, despite the fact that some of their most valued contributors blossomed as muckrakers in other journals, it is even more important to emphasize the mass circulation of those other journals. A low-price magazine which could vault to a circulation of nearly half a million in a country with, at the turn of the century, little better than a third its present population — and with a substantial proportion of newly arrived immigrants and native illiterates — was obviously saying something of value to millions of Americans. When we multiply this by the total number of magazines whose circulations were zooming upwards because they were encouraging and publishing the muckraking writers; when we remind ourselves that there were at the time no true picture magazines, no television, no radio, no movies, we begin to sense that we are

here witnessing the birth of the modern mass media (the parallel — but distinct — development of yellow journalism is one which cannot be examined here). Isn't it worth pondering the fact that the mass magazine was born of this arousal of the American conscience by a band of bold editors making common cause with novelists, poets, and litterateurs?

In his brilliant early book, *The Golden Day*, Lewis Mumford makes what seems to me a most telling argument against overvaluing the ultimate impact of the muckrakers. "In attack, in criticism," he says, "they did able work; but when it came to offering a genuine alternative, their picture became a negative one: industry without millionaires, cities without graft, art without luxury, love without sordid calculation. They were ready to upset every aspect of modern industrial society except the fragmentary culture which had brought it into existence."

Mr. Mumford goes on to point out a truth which the thirty-five years since he first committed it to paper have only strengthened — that capitalism itself *can* provide what it was attacked for not providing, and that the real indictment of it lies elsewhere: "the essential poverty of America was a qualitative poverty, one which cut through the divisions of rich and poor; and it has been this sort of poverty which has prevented us from projecting in the imagination a more excellent society. Life was more complicated in America but not more significant; life was richer in material goods but not in creative energies. These eager and relentless journalists were unaware of the necessity for establishing different kinds of goods than the existing ones; they had no notion of other values, other modes, other forms of activity than those practiced by the society around them."

Anyone who reads the literature, not the journalism, produced by the muck-

rakers, must be persuaded of the just-
ness of Mr. Mumford's reproach. Those
reformers who, like Brand Whitlock, invested all their indignation as well as all
their creative energy not in journalism
but in novel writing, produced books
which, despite the polite references to
them by American historians, are all but
unreadable today. Those who divided
their energies between poetry and muckraking — Edwin Markham, Ernest Crosby,
Charles Edward Russell — produced poetry which is now hardly recalled even
by specialists in the period. . . .

Writing in the *Cosmopolitan* in 1906,
Upton Sinclair, still flushed with the fan-
tastic success of *The Jungle*, spelled out
the reasons why the opening chapters of
that bombshell of a book were (and still
are) so explosively charged; at the same
time he unconsciously exposed the roots
of an aesthetic misconception that was to
strangulate not only his own later fiction,
but also much of the work of Sherwood
Anderson and of the proletarian writers
of the 1930's:

In many respects I had Uncle Tom's Cabin
in mind as a model of what I wished to do.
. . . But now there is a stirring of life within
the masses themselves. The proletarian
writer is beginning to find a voice, and also
an audience and a means of support. And
he does not find the life of his fellows a
fascinating opportunity for feats of artistry;
he finds it a nightmare inferno, a thing
whose one conceivable excellence is that it
drives men to rebellion and to mutual aid in
escaping. The proletarian writer is a writer
with a purpose; he thinks no more of "art
for art's sake" than a man on a sinking ship
thinks of painting a beautiful picture in the
cabin; he thinks of getting ashore, and of
getting his brothers and comrades ashore —
and then there will be time enough for art.
. . . So far as I myself am concerned, the well-
springs of joy and beauty have been dried up
in me — the flowers no longer sing to me as

they used to, nor the sunrise, nor the stars;
I have become like a soldier upon a hard
campaign — I am thinking only of the enemy.
The experiences of my life have been such
that I cannot think of them without turning
sick; there is no way that I can face the
thought of them at all, save as being practice
for the writing of *The Jungle*. I see that it
was necessary that some one should have
had such experiences, in order that it might
be impossible for any man to have them
again.

Regardless of whether the novelist
blocked his own development by imag-
ining himself a soldier rather than an
artist, or whether (as seems most likely
in those whom we are considering) he
simply lacked the necessary imaginative
gifts from the very outset, the unhappy
fact remains that the literary efforts of
the muckrakers were not on a par with
their journalistic labors.

But what of these labors? Can one go
along with Lewis Mumford when he
concludes: "For all the effect that these
painstaking pictures had in lifting the
worker onto a more active plane of manhood, one would willingly trade the
whole literature for a handful of good
songs. . . ."?

Seldom if ever has the craft of journalism more responsibly served the individual conscience and the national interest. The ardent American notion of a free
society, freely inclusive, freely elected,
and freely helpful, had been cynically
shoved aside in the closing decades of
the nineteenth century. If it was revivified in the early years of the new century, to the benefit of every American
who has come of age since then, that
must be credited in substantial measure
to the ringing voices of the muckrakers,
recalling their fellow citizens to an honest understanding of their responsibilities
and their potentialities in a democratic
society.

IV. MUCKRAKING AND THE PATTERN OF PROGRESSIVE REFORM

Vernon Louis Parrington: A CHAPTER IN AMERICAN LIBERALISM

Vernon Louis Parrington's Main Currents in American Thought *is a classic account of the clash of the liberal and conservative traditions in American society. Parrington evaluates the success of the muckrakers in altering American public opinion to the realities of early twentieth century capitalism.*

THE great movement of liberalism that took possession of the American mind after the turn of the century — a movement not unworthy to be compared with the ferment of the eighteen forties — was the spontaneous reaction of an America still only half urbanized, still clinging to ideals and ways of an older simpler America, to an industrialism that was driving its plowshare through the length and breadth of the familiar scene, turning under the rude furrows what before had been growing familiarly there. It was the first reaction of America to the revolutionary change that followed upon the exhaustion of the frontier — an attempt to secure through the political state the freedoms that before had come from unpreempted opportunity.

For a quarter of a century following the great westward expansion of the late sixties, America had been drifting heedlessly towards a different social order. The shambling frontier democracy that had sufficed an earlier time was visibly breaking down in presence of the imperious power of a centralizing capitalism.

The railways were a dramatic embodiment of the new machine civilization that was running head on into a primitive social organism fashioned by the old domestic economy, and the disruptions and confusions were a warning that the country was in for vast changes. New masters, new ways. The rule of the captain of industry had come. The farmers had long been in an ugly mood, but their great rebellion was put down in 1896, and never again could they hope to wrest sovereignty from capitalism. The formal adoption of the gold standard in 1900 served notice to the world that America had put away its democratic agrarianism, that a shambling Jacksonian individualism had had its day, and that henceforth the destiny of the country lay in the hands of its business men. Capitalism was master of the country and though for the present it was content to use the political machinery of democracy it was driving towards an objective that was the negation of democracy.

The immediate reaction to so broad a shift in the course of manifest destiny was a growing uneasiness amongst the middle class — small business and professional men — who looked with fear upon the program of the captains of industry. Industrialization brought its jars and upsets. The little fish did not enjoy being swallowed by the big, and as they watched the movement of economic centralization encroaching on the field of competition they saw the doors of opportunity closing to them. It was to this great body of *petite bourgeoisie* that members of the lesser intellectuals — journalists, sociologists, reformers — were to make appeal. The work was begun dramatically with the spectacularly advertised *Frenzied Finance*, written by Thomas W. Lawson, and appearing as a series in *McClure's Magazine* in 1903. The immense popular success of the venture proved that the fire was ready for the fat, and at once a host of volunteer writers fell to feeding the flames. The new ten-cent magazines provided the necessary vehicle of publicity, and enterprising editors were soon increasing their circulations with every issue. As it became evident how popular was the chord that had been struck, more competent workmen joined themselves to the group of journalists: a growing army of them — essayists, historians, political scientists, philosophers, a host of heavy-armed troops that moved forward in a frontal attack on the strongholds of the new plutocracy. Few writers in the years between 1903 and 1917 escaped being drawn into the movement — an incorrigible romantic perhaps, like the young James Branch Cabell, or a cool patrician like Edith Wharton; and with such popular novelists as Winston Churchill, Robert Herrick, Ernest Poole, David Graham Phillips, Upton Sinclair, and Jack London embellishing the rising liberalism with dramatic heroes and villains, and dressing their salads with the wickedness of Big Business; with such political leaders as Bob La Follette and Theodore Roosevelt and Woodrow Wilson beating up the remotest villages for recruits; with such scholars as Thorstein Veblen, Charles A. Beard, and John Dewey, and such lawyers as Louis Brandeis, Frank P. Walsh, and Samuel Untermyer, the movement gathered such momentum and quickened such a ferment as had not been known before in the land since the days of the Abolition controversy. The mind and conscience of America were stirred to their lowest sluggish stratum, and a democratic renaissance was all aglow on the eastern horizon.

At the core it was a critical realistic movement that spread quietly among intellectuals, but the nebulous tail of the comet blazed across the sky for all to wonder at: and it was the tail rather than the core that aroused the greatest immediate interest. Lincoln Steffens, Charles Edward Russell, Ida Tarbell, Gustavus Myers, and Upton Sinclair were read eagerly because they dealt with themes that many were interested in — the political machine, watered stock, Standard Oil, the making of great fortunes, and the like — and they invested their exposures with the dramatic interest of a detective story. Up to 1910 it was largely a muckraking movement — to borrow President Roosevelt's picturesque phrase; a time of brisk housecleaning that searched out old cobwebs and disturbed the dust that lay thick on the antiquated furniture. The Gilded Age had been slovenly and such a housecleaning was long overdue. There was a vast amount of nosing about to discover bad smells, and to sensitive noses the bad smells seemed to be everywhere. Evidently some hidden cesspool was fouling American life, and as the inquisitive plumbers tested the household drains they came upon the source of infection — not one cesspool but many, under every city hall and beneath every state capitol — dug secretly by politicians in the pay of respectable business men. It was these cesspools that were poisoning the national household, and there would be no health in America till they were filled in and no others dug.

It was a dramatic discovery and when the corruption of American politics was laid on the threshold of business — like a bastard on the doorsteps of the father — a tremendous disturbance resulted. There was a great fluttering and clamor amongst the bats and owls, an ominous creaking of the machine as the wrenches were thrown into the well-oiled wheels, and a fierce sullen anger at the hue and cry set up. To many honest Americans the years between 1903 and 1910 were abusive and scurrilous beyond decency, years when no man and no business, however honorable, was safe from the pillory; when wholesale exposure had grown profitable to sensation-mongers, and great reputations were lynched by vigilantes and reputable corporations laid under indictment at the bar of public opinion. Respectable citizens did not like to have their goodly city held up to the world as "corrupt and contented"; they did not like to have their municipal housekeeping brought into public disrepute no matter how sluttish it might be. It was not pleasant for members of great families to read a cynical history of the origins of their fortunes, or for railway presidents seeking political favors to find on the newsstand a realistic account of the bad scandals that had smirched their roads. It was worse than unpleasant, it was hurtful to business. And so quietly and as speedily as could

be done decently, the movement was brought to a stop by pressure put on the magazines that lent themselves to such harmful disclosures. Then followed a campaign of education. Responding to judicious instruction, conducted in the columns of the most respectable newspapers, the American public was soon brought to understand that it was not the muck that was harmful, but the indiscretion of those who commented in print on the bad smells. It was reckoned a notable triumph for sober and patriotic good sense.

So after a few years of amazing activity the muckraking movement came to a stop. But not before it had done its work; not before the American middle class had been indoctrinated in the elementary principles of political realism and had rediscovered the social conscience lost since the days of the Civil War. Many a totem had been thrown down by the irreverent hands of the muckrakers, and many a fetish held up to ridicule, and plutocracy in America would not recover its peace of mind until at great cost the totems should be set up again and the fetishes reanointed with the oil of sanctity. The substantial result of the movement was the instruction it afforded in the close kinship between business and politics — a lesson greatly needed by a people long fed on romantic unrealities. It did not crystallize for the popular mind in the broad principle of economic determinism; that remained for certain of the intellectuals to apply to American experience. But with its sordid object — service — it punished the flabby optimism of the Gilded Age, with its object-lessons in business politics; it revealed the hidden hand that was pulling the strings of the political puppets; it tarnished the gilding that had been carefully laid on our callous exploitation, and it brought under

common suspicion the captain of industry who had risen as a national hero from
the muck of individualism. It was a sharp
guerrilla attack on the sacred American

System, but behind the thin skirmish-line
lay a volunteer army that was making
ready to deploy for a general engagement with plutocracy.

C. C. Regier: THE BALANCE SHEET

Cornelius C. Regier's The Era of the Muckrakers (1932) *was a pioneer study of the reform journalists. Until this work appeared, historians had paid scant attention to the muckraking movement. In the
last chapter, "The Balance Sheet," Regier summarizes his appraisal of
muckraking and considers various explanations of the movement's
decline.*

IT IS clear that muckraking is not
something that was discovered by a
group of men in the first decade of the
twentieth century. What does distinguish that decade is the fact that there
then existed a muckraking movement, a
concerted effort on the part of a large
number of writers, using as their medium
books and pamphlets but more especially the popular magazines which had
sprung up in the late eighties and early
nineties and had, by the turn of the century, achieved large circulations. Muckraking, as a movement, began late in
1902, became militant in 1903, in 1904
and 1905, and by 1906 was a force that
was felt throughout the nation. By 1908
it was dying down, but the Taft administration revived the interest in the literature of exposure and gave a new incen-
tive to the cause of liberalism in politics.
The activities of the insurgents in Congress in 1909 and 1910 provided a center
for agitation, and the tariff legislation

enacted at that time proved a source of
dissatisfaction and a subject for criticism.
In 1911 muckraking was again at a high
point, and many of the muckrakers par-
ticipated in the campaign of 1912. But
even before that three-cornered struggle,
muckraking was again on the decrease,
and soon nothing was left that could be
described as a movement. Some writers
and some magazines continued to expose
corruption and vice, but whatever frag-
ments of the movement remained were
crushed by the entrance of this country
into the war. Since the World War, attempts to revive muckraking have largely
proved abortive, and "debunking" was
for a time the only popular form of the
literature of exposure.

Looking back on the muckraking
movement, we can readily see that it was
part of a larger social, intellectual, and
political development. In the nineties,
as was pointed out, the average man ac-
quiesced in the methods of industry and

From C. C. Regier, *The Era of the Muckrakers* (Chapel Hill, 1932), pp. 194–214. Reprinted by
permission of the University of North Carolina Press.

commerce. Industrial expansion seemed as much a matter of "manifest destiny" as geographical expansion had seemed in the days before the Civil War, and no more thought was given to those who were ruined by the ruthless methods of the business men than had been wasted on the Indians and Mexicans whose land was taken from them. For the poor there was sympathy and even charity, but few people stopped to consider the conditions which made poverty inevitable. The majority threw themselves into the struggle for wealth with as little consideration for abstract theories of right and wrong as the pioneers had shown in the struggle for land. Even those who were beaten in the struggle were inclined to look upon their defeat as produced by the very laws of nature, and not through the operation of controllable social forces.

Of course there were movements of protest in the nineties, but it was not until the next decade that there came a definite revolt against Big Business. Gradually, but on the whole with surprising rapidity, people, partly because of the facts which the muckrakers revealed, partly because of the visions of better things which the reformers held before them, partly because of chastening personal experiences, began to regard the corporations as enemies rather than as friends. In particular, the comfortable middle classes, who had viewed the earlier stages of the growth of monopoly with considerable complacency, now began to fear the power of the trusts. And they turned to the government as their bulwark in the struggle against the great interests. Formerly, they had accepted the view that the function of government was to protect and encourage the growth of business enterprise; now they demanded that the state and federal legislatures enact laws which would defend the rights of the common people by restraining the activities of the large corporations.

It is significant that there came to be much talk about the "social conscience." Forward-looking men in the churches and in public life began to say that too much attention had been paid to the sins of the individual. They pointed out that men who were kindly, thoughtful, and high-principled in their private lives condoned and even practised business methods which brought poverty, misery, and disease to millions. Washington Gladden noted our discovery that no society could march hellward faster than a democracy under the banner of unbridled individualism. A "Golden Rule" movement was started in 1901, and it was the intention of the founders that the Golden Rule should be practised in business and political relations. Dr. Max Farrand holds that every twenty or thirty years a wave of "moral hysteria" passes over the country, and practices that were once regarded as proper and honorable come to be condemned and scorned. "Hysteria" may or may not be the right word, but it is true that, with almost the suddenness of conversion, the attitude of the American people toward industry and toward government underwent a complete reversal.

The expression of the attitude was twofold: exposure and reform. It is important to note that, taking the most conservative figures available, those given in Ayer's *American Newspaper Annual and Directory*, we find the total circulation of the ten magazines which engaged in muckraking to run over three million. These periodicals devoted a considerable proportion of their space, sometimes as much as 20 per cent, to articles of exposure. And in addition to the magazines we have books and the newspapers. Several of Russell's books sold more than thirty thousand copies, and both *The Brass Check* and *The Jungle* went over the hundred thousand mark. A few newspapers, particularly the New York *World* and the Kansas City *Star*, aided materially in the campaign. We have every reason, then, to suppose that the muckrakers touched in one way or another the great majority of American citizens.

Parallel with the muckraking movement went a political movement which took shape in a variety of ways. Some of the muckrakers were Socialists, but others, probably the majority, believed that the capitalistic system could be so altered as to meet the needs of the nation. During the Roosevelt administration the hopes of the liberals were pinned on the President, and much of the legislation for which he was responsible met with their approval. With the Taft administration reaction set in, and the liberals linked themselves with the insurgents in Congress. In 1912 the liberal movement was divided. Many of the men who had worked for reform supported Roosevelt and the Progressive party, but others gave their allegiance to Wilson and "The New Freedom" of which he eloquently spoke and wrote. But at no time from 1902 to 1912 were the muckrakers and the reformers without some political figure who seemed to embody more or less adequately the ideals which they held.

Since Roosevelt was the outstanding statesman of the muckraking era, and since he was intimately associated with many of the measures which were intended to remedy the evil situations which the muckrakers exposed, it is interesting to note the judgments expressed in 1922 by some of the leaders. Mr. S. S. McClure, in a letter to the present writer, stated:

President Roosevelt was the most influential force in getting good things done that the country ever possessed. He assisted all good causes and hindered all bad causes.

William Allen White expressed a similar opinion:

Roosevelt was the leader of the liberal movement. At the famous Gridiron Dinner in which Roosevelt spoke about the muckrakers, Uncle Joe Cannon spoke up, and said, "Yes, you're the chief muckraker," which was literally true.

More critical was the verdict of Ray Stannard Baker:

In the beginning I thought, and still think, he did great good in giving support and encouragement to this movement. But I did not believe then, and have never believed since, that these ills can be settled by partisan political methods. They are moral and economic questions. Latterly I believe Roosevelt did a disservice to the country in seizing upon a movement that ought to have been built up slowly and solidly from the bottom with much solid thought and experimentation, and hitching it to the cart of his own political ambitions. He thus short-circuited a fine and vigorous current of aroused public opinion into a futile partisan movement.

John S. Phillips and Charles Edward Russell went even further. The former wrote:

The greatest single definite force against muckraking was President Roosevelt, who called these writers muckrakers. A tag like that running through the papers was an easy phrase of repeated attack upon what was in general a good journalistic movement.

And Russell, when asked what place Roosevelt had in the muckraking movement, replied:

None of any honor. He did much to hamper and discourage it, but never a thing to help it. His speech in which he first misapplied . . . a passage of Bunyan to this work of righteousness, frightened some timid editors and greatly emboldened those malefactors of great wealth to whom he was afterward supposed to be hostile.

But the fact remains, whatever individual muckrakers may think of Roosevelt, that muckraking was closely bound up with the progressive movement for reform, and that both movements were expressions of the attitude of the decade. It was a period not merely of bitter criticism but also of high hopes. The liberals of the period felt that they were getting results, and that they would go on getting results. It seemed as if a new Golden Age were at hand, not only for American business and government, but also for American letters and art. Much of the writing of the nineties, as already observed, was infinitely removed from the realities of life, but the authors of the early nineteen-hundreds were eager to grapple with American problems and to find their subjects on American soil. Robert Herrick, in a series of novels on the American scene, criticized the shallowness and crassness of his contemporaries, especially the women. Theodore Dreiser was beginning his distinguished career. William Allen White's immensely popular *A Certain Rich Man* (1909), portrayed the growth of the Middle West since the Civil War, ending on a note of high optimism and ardent faith. Brand Whitlock was writing about politics; Winston Churchill shifted from historical romances to critical studies of politics, business, and the church; Edith Wharton was achieving realistic works of distinction. In American literature, especially in the novel, a new spirit was evident: a determination to utilize typi-

cally American material; a willingness to criticize unflinchingly what was unseemly in American life; a note of confidence in America's future.

. . . [I]t is quite possible to argue that the whole tone of business in the United States was raised because of the persistent exposure of corruption and injustice. As early as 1909 John Forbes stated that in his early business career "things were done without a thought of their being wrong that the public would not for an instant stand for to-day." The Rev. Hugh Black declared in 1922, "during the sixteen years that I have been in America the whole basis of commercial morality has changed." In 1921, Dr. Frank C. Doan, comparing the public attitude a quarter-century ago with that of his own time, said that whereas old men had once advised him to rid himself of his dreams of social justice, he found intelligent men everywhere willing to listen to talk of the Sermon on the Mount and the Golden Rule. Even Charles Edward Russell, who has remained militant in his attitude, believes that business methods have been remade, that the old tactics of monopoly have been abandoned, that business has been humanized and made decent so far as that is possible under our competitive system, that there is a general interest in the conditions of labor, and that competitors are no longer put out of business without regard to law. President Wilson, in his message to Congress in January, 1914, summarized an opinion that was widely held when he said, "At last the masters of business on the great scale have begun to yield their preference and their purpose, and perhaps their judgment also, in honorable surrender." One of the most impressive statements on the subject is to be found in an article entitled "Higher Standards Developing in

American Business," written by Judge Elbert H. Gary, and published in *Current History* for March, 1926. Judge Gary, after contrasting the business ethics of to-day with the practices current twenty-five years ago, writes:

To my personal knowledge many men of big affairs have completely changed their opinions and methods concerning ethical questions in business. The majority of business men conduct operations on the basis that right is superior to might; that morality is on a par with legality and the observance of both is essential to worthy achievement. They regard employees as associates and partners instead of servants. Executives have come to understand that stockholders are entitled to any reasonable information, so that under no circumstances can there be preferential rights and opportunities. At last it has been perceived — and this belief is spreading everywhere — that destructive competition must give way to humane competition; that the Golden Rule is not an empty phrase, but a golden principle. Finally, business as a whole sees that full and prompt publicity of all facts involving the public weal, not only must be made possible, but must be insisted upon as a primary tenet of good faith.

It is something to have great industrialists and financiers rendering even lip-service to ethical principles and humane considerations.

The achievements of muckraking and the liberal movement in the field of legislative accomplishments can be more easily tabulated. The list of reforms accomplished between 1900 and 1915 is an impressive one. The convict and peonage systems were destroyed in some states; prison reforms were undertaken; a federal pure food act was passed in 1906; child labor laws were adopted by many states; a federal employers' liability act was passed in 1906, and a second one in 1908, which was amended in 1910; forest reserves were set aside; the Newlands Act of 1902 made reclamation of millions of acres of land possible; a policy of the conservation of natural resources was followed; eight-hour laws for women were passed in some states; race-track gambling was prohibited; twenty states passed mothers' pension acts between 1908 and 1913; twenty-five states had workmen's compensation laws in 1915; a tariff commission was established in 1909, abolished in 1912, and revived in 1914; an income tax amendment was added to the Constitution; the Standard Oil and the Tobacco companies were dissolved; Niagara Falls was saved from the greed of corporations; Alaska was saved from the Guggenheims and other capitalists; and better insurance laws and packing-house laws were placed on the statute books. Some changes can be traced directly to specific muckraking articles. *Hampton's* maintained that Charles Edward Russell's articles on the Southern Pacific Railroad were instrumental in breaking the power of that corporation in California politics. Mr. Russell himself states that the articles of John L. Mathews were responsible for defeating the plans of the Water Power Trust. And it is fairly clear that it was because of Russell's articles that Trinity Church destroyed the vile and unsanitary tenements from which it had long been drawing income.

The period also witnessed a number of important changes in the machinery of government: the popular election of United States senators, direct legislation through the initiative, referendum, and recall, direct primaries, corrupt practices acts, campaign expense laws, commission form of government for cities, and woman suffrage — reforms all of which were intended to remedy the abuses pointed out by the muckrakers. William Allen White, in 1909, stated that the shackles of democracy — direct bribery, party bribery, machine rule, and unresponsive legislative control of the states — had been thrown off. The muckrakers probably deserve credit also for the introduction of congressional investigations, for the development of sociological surveys, for the devising of methods of popular exposition which the later essayists and the conservative magazines adopted, and for the destruction of the awe and reverence in which wealth had been held. *Everybody's*, in 1909, offered a somewhat exuberant summary of what had been accomplished:

Wall Street cannot gull the public as it once did. Insurance is on a sounder basis. Banking is adding new safeguards. Advertising is nearly honest. Rebating is unsafe. Food and drug adulteration are dangerous. Human life is more respected by common carriers. The hour of the old-time political boss is struck. States and municipalities are insisting upon clean administrators. The people are naming their own candidates. Independent voters, and that means thinking men, are legion. The children are having their day in court. Protection is offered to the weak against the gambling shark and saloon. Our public resources are being conserved. The public health is being considered. New standards of life have been raised up. The money god totters. Patriotism, manhood, brotherhood are exalted. It is a new era. A new world. Good signs, don't you think? And what has brought it about? Muckraking. Bless your heart, just plain muckraking. By magazine writers and newspapers and preachers and public men and Roosevelt.

We may discount as much as we like the enthusiasm of the editor of *Everybody's* and of other commentators on the achievements of the era, but it still remains obvious, even from so cursory a survey as we have offered, that a great many important and valuable reforms were adopted, as the result, in part at least, of muckraking. What the muckrakers tried to do was necessary; the evils were there, and there was no hope of removing them until the public was aroused to a recognition of their existence. What they accomplished was significant; the public was aroused and conditions were improved. Why, then, did muckraking cease?

The first, and most obvious answer, in view of what has just been said, is that muckraking was no longer needed because the conditions against which it was directed had been abolished. This seems plausible enough, and there is indeed some truth in it. The more flagrant evils, both in politics and in industry, had been eliminated. Moreover, the public had been aroused, and Congress, together with the state legislatures, was carrying on investigations of its own and was apparently committed to a policy of reform. On the other hand, in 1911, when muckraking ceased, many important reforms, some of which were adopted during the first Wilson administration, were still unrealized, and, furthermore, it was already apparent that many of the old evils were appearing in new guises. Monopoly had been abolished in theory, but it still existed in fact. Despite the amendment providing for direct election, senators were frequently chosen by the same old bosses. The direct primary, for which so much had been hoped, was proving a disappointment in many states. Business might be less open in its defiance of law, but there were many subtle ways of evading legislation that clamored for exposure. Finally, it is to be noted that many of the muckrakers were themselves dissatisfied with what had been achieved while the liberals in politics put forth their greatest efforts in 1912, a year in which there was almost no muckraking. Quite probably belief that muckraking was no longer needed had something to do with the decline of public interest in exposure, a point which will be discussed shortly, but it is wrong to suggest that the muckrakers ceased their efforts of their own accord because they believed that their work was finished.

We must go on, then, to discuss other factors in the cessation of muckraking, and immediately there comes to mind another possibility: perhaps muckraking did not stop; perhaps it was stopped. We have repeatedly commented on the extent to which muckraking was made possible by the rise of the popular magazines, and we have already seen, in the chapter on the press, that a number of muckraking magazines were forced out of existence or compelled to change their policies. It is difficult to analyze the facts, but as already seen, there is considerable evidence to show that financial interests did manage to suppress more than one magazine that had been antagonistic to Big Business.

William Allen White, however, believes it was a "natural phenomenon" that the liberal magazines should fall into the hands of their creditors, mostly financiers, when liberalism declined and with it the popularity of these periodicals. He writes, "There is absolutely no truth in the story that there was a deliberate plot on the part of the great financial interests to grab the magazines." And we have, in support of his position, the fact that the costs of publishing had greatly increased, making advertising necessary if magazines were to survive.

To the present writer it seems possible to find much truth in both these statements. To him the evidence seems overwhelming that some muckraking magazines, which might otherwise have survived for some time longer, were deliberately and ruthlessly put out of business by the interests which they had antagonized. On the other hand, it is reasonable to suppose that these magazines could have continued, in defiance of the financiers, if the public interest in muckraking had been maintained and circulation had remained large. And it is quite clear that other magazines gave up muckraking, not because their existence was threatened by the financiers and industrialists, but because articles devoted to exposure did not serve to sell copies. Financial pressure may have hastened the demise of muckraking, but there is no conclusive evidence that it was a case of murder in the first degree.

We come inevitably, then, to the conclusion that muckraking ceased, primarily, because the American people were tired of it. John S. Phillips, in a letter to the author, states:

This phase of journalism died down because of the unwarranted and exaggerated imitations done without study and containing much that was untrue. The result of these things was a revulsion and a loss of public interest. Journalistically, the scheme was given up because readers didn't want to read that sort of thing any more. The same thing happened in the political field. Victor Murdock and Senator Beveridge both told me they couldn't get any response to the former kind of speech. The people at large, as readers and auditors, are changeable and when they get tired of a certain kind of thing they stop reading and stop attending lectures and speeches.

John O'Hara Cosgrave, editor of *Everybody's* during the muckraking period, says much the same thing: "The subject was not exhausted but the public interest therein seemed to be at an end, and inevitably the editors turned to other sources for copy to fill their pages."

But why the change in public interest? Why, indeed? Why does public interest permit one play to run on Broadway for five years, while another, and a much better, according to the critics, dies in its first week? Why does public interest send this book, rather than that, to the head of the list of best-sellers? Why did the public interest in muckraking ever develop? These questions cannot be conclusively answered, for public taste is largely incalculable. "The wind bloweth where it listeth." But, even as we tried to show some of the reasons for the beginning of public interest, so we can now seek a partial explanation for its decline.

In the first place, as already suggested, it is possible that many people believed so many important reforms had taken place that there was no need for muckraking. In the second place, it may be that the excitement wore off in time, with the result that the magazine readers found more of a thrill in stories about cowboys and bandits than they did in articles about senators and industrialists. In the third place, as Mr. Phillips says, the increased sensationalism of the latter years of the era may have sickened people with the whole business. In the fourth place, intelligent citizens may have become impatient with exposure and may have begun to demand what they should do to remedy conditions. And, in the fifth place, the mere fact that muckraking had gone on for ten years may be enough to explain why the reading public was weary of it.

We come, in short, to the conclusion that to a considerable extent muckraking was little more than a fad. Many writers took up muckraking because, for the time being, it was more profitable than other forms of writing. They gave up writing pretty romances, western thrillers, or ingenious yarns about detectives, in order to "expose" real or imagined abuses. Naturally they turned to other fields the moment it seemed likely that greater profit lay therein. Some of the editors were much the same. They had little of the social vision which brought the *Arena, McClure's, Collier's,* and *Hampton's,* to mention without invidious intent only a few names, into the muckraking campaign. They sought only to capitalize a tendency of the times. Such writers and such editors, of course, did not hesitate over sensationalism, and accuracy was of only minor concern. By their attitude and their conduct they did much to bring muckraking into discredit, and when the public would have no more of it, they blithely turned to other things.

We have said enough, perhaps, to explain why muckraking ended, but it is important to devote a little more attention to those writers who were both purposeful and competent, to those periodicals whose editors were sincerely devoted to the general good, to that section of the public which examined with seriousness and intelligence the literature of exposure. Probably the decline of muckraking was hastened by the insincerity of certain writers and editors, the cheapness of what they wrote and published, and the superficiality of the interest they aroused. But we should study the movement at its best, noting the criticisms which have been directed against it, and endeavoring to discover if there were inherent weaknesses that may have contributed to its cessation.

It has been frequently charged that the muckrakers were not fundamental enough in their diagnoses and in their prescriptions. Walter Lippmann, for example, in *Drift and Mastery* (1914), charges the muckrakers with failing to understand the great changes in American life. They did not realize how the nature of industry had been altered, and they were content to denounce this abuse and remedy that evil without ever touching the bases of the whole problem. William Archer reached a similar conclusion, declaring in his article on "The American Cheap Magazine" that the muckrakers were never willing to admit that collectivism was the only permanent check upon the enslavement of the people by the most amazing plutocracy the world had ever seen. Frederic C. Howe, in his *Confessions of a Reformer* (1925), argues that the whole liberal movement was on the wrong basis. The liberals thought that it was enough to make people see what was wrong; they did not realize that the mind "refused to work against economic interest."

In all these criticisms there is more than a grain of truth. Of course it cannot be said that all the muckrakers were afraid of collectivism, for Sinclair and Russell, and at one time Lincoln Steffens, were Socialists. But most of the muckrakers described themselves as "liberals," meaning by that term much or little, as the case might be, and even the Socialists did not seem fully to understand how their dogmas were to be applied to American life. As Lippmann has said, the muckrakers were not leaders, showing men and women how to rise above the chaos of individualistic industrialism; they were, rather, symptoms and expressions of that chaos. Their exposures were unquestionably fruitful, but more than muckraking was necessary for healing the sores of American civilization. Of far-reaching and fundamental philosophy the muckrakers had little; as a result their movement could be only a passing phase in the long struggle for justice and liberty.

Other criticisms have been leveled against these men. It has been charged that the muckrakers were not sufficiently accurate and painstaking in their studies, and that their articles consisted of rhetoric instead of facts. This was true of the more sensational muckrakers, but it was not true of the revolutionary exposures made by such investigators as Steffens, Tarbell, Baker, Connolly, and their confreres. John S. Phillips, who served on both *McClure's* and the *American,* says: "So thorough was the work then, that, although we dealt with libelous materials all the time, there was only one suit for libel sustained against the magazine [*McClure's*]." And this suit was successful simply because a document on which an article was based turned out to be inaccurate.

It is amazing, when one considers the kind of material these men were using, how few successful libel suits were brought against them. A single article might blast a political reputation or ruin a business. Naturally, the people who were attacked sued for damages if they dared. Samuel Hopkins Adams says that he was threatened with suit after suit but usually all he needed to do was to point out that he had far more information than he had thus far used, and the threat was forgotten. Of all the threats produced by his patent medicine articles, comparatively few materialized into cases, and of these cases he lost but one. Will Irwin had six suits filed against him, but only one was brought to trial. Connolly, as already mentioned, filed a suit for libel himself and won it. Steffens, despite the fact that he was constantly destroying the prestige of eminent politicians, never had to pay a cent in damages. The victims of muckraking were on the lookout for the slightest inaccuracy and yet the muckrakers lost very few cases.

This is some indication of the reliability of the better type of muckraking, but there are other proofs. We have already mentioned the time and money expended in preparing some of the series, and have called attention to the fact that many articles were based entirely on official documents. It should also be noted that articles were subjected to the most rigorous editorial scrutiny, and that the advice of experts was occasionally obtained. In the better type of muckraking, matters of hearsay were entirely eliminated, and merely personal charges were never included. Of course there were muckrakers who were reckless, and there were muckrakers who could not distinguish between evidence and rumor, but the general level of accuracy in the leading magazines was astoundingly high.

If we wish to find other criticisms of the movement, criticisms many of which were voiced by men who took part in it, we need only turn to the *Survey Graphic* for February, 1926, in which are printed twenty-three answers to the question, "Where are the pre-war radicals?", raised by Mr. Howe in his *Confessions of a Reformer*. The criticisms contained in these statements are directed against the liberal movement, but some of them apply to muckraking. Stuart Chase pleads for a more careful study of facts, declaring that "the Uplift . . . is comatose if not completely ossified — strangled both by the war and its own ineptitude. It was inept because its moral judgments took the place of sound analysis." Ray Stannard Baker says that he and his fellows were on the wrong track because they believed that what they wanted could be had by "adopting certain easy devices or social inventions," and he insists that more understanding is necessary. "Think of us," he writes, "as having gone back to get acquainted with life; of liking better for a while to ask questions than to answer them; of *trying to understand.*" And William Hard says that the liberals have depended too much on legislation and political reform, not realizing that to create a bureaucracy is to put a weapon into the hands of the classes they are trying to fight.

These criticisms all point to the conclusion stated a moment ago: muckraking, however necessary and however valuable it might have been for the time being, was essentially a superficial attack upon a problem which demanded — and demands — fundamental analysis and treatment. If we paraphrase Mr. Howe's provocative question and ask ourselves "Where are the pre-war muckrakers?" we are likely to find some indication of what happened to the movement.

We see, in the first place, that the spirit of many of these men remains unchanged. Upton Sinclair is still a muckraker, but, until very recently, he has found it necessary to publish his own books in order to get them before the public. Charles Edward Russell also remains critical, but, unable or unwilling to follow Sinclair's example, he has failed to secure a medium through which his political and social ideas could reach the reading public. Thus these two writers illustrate the influence which economic pressure has had in checking the movement.

Others of the old muckrakers are engaged in what is a modern approximation of muckraking. Will Irwin has done important service in his exposures of the horrors and the futility of war and in his articles on the scandal in the Veterans' Bureau. Samuel Hopkins Adams, devoting himself chiefly to fiction and writing under a pseudonym as well as under his own name, has used one of his novels, *Revelry*, in order to make a startling exposure of the Harding regime. And George Creel, writing for *Collier's* under the name of "Uncle Henry," frequently offers friendly but acidulous criticisms of things-as-they-are.

In one way or another, the muckrakers have adapted themselves to the changes that have taken place in the life of the nation. The transformation which brought us David Grayson in place of Ray Stannard Baker is significant because it reveals Baker's belief that we must have understanding, and Baker's present devotion to the history of the Wilson administration still further illuminates his decision that quiet study rather than noisy assertion is the present need. Mark Sullivan, though writing on politics, seems to have tempered his views, and he, too, is devoting himself to history. Ida M. Tarbell, apparently, has made an even more drastic change; at least her life of Judge Gary shocked those readers who remembered with approval her history of the Standard Oil Company. Steffens, after a long stay in Europe, is back in this country and, as mentioned above, has just published his *Autobiography*. He has come to the conclusion that the movement toward union of big business with politics is inevitable. Like an old contented lover he accepts conditions as they are. "I have been contending," he writes, "with all my kind, always against God. . . . The world which I tried so hard, so honestly, so dumbly, to change has changed me. . . . And as for the world in general, all that was or is or ever will be wrong with that is my — our thinking about it." Then there are some of the muckrakers who, like the late Thomas Lawson, went scurrying back to the swine and their husks.

Because muckraking was to some extent merely a fad — of which the public grew tired, because of the pressure of financial interests, because some of the evils exposed had been remedied, and because of inherent weakness in the movement itself, muckraking came to an end. Even liberalism, of which muckraking was but a part, received a stunning blow when the United States entered the World War.

John Chamberlain: THE MUCK-RAKE PACK

In Farewell to Reform *(1932) John Chamberlain traced "the rise, life and decay of the progressive mind in America." This book reflected the alienation of radical intellectuals during the 1930's from the earlier reform tradition. The chapter devoted to muckraking sketches the history of the movement and offers a judgement of the journalists' success in solving social problems.*

Copyright © 1932 by John Chamberlain. Reprinted from *Farewell to Reform,* pp. 122–143, by John Chamberlain. By permission of The John Day Company, Inc., publisher.

W. J. GHENT'S prognosis of a benevolent feudalism was not, it must be admitted, an act of pure divination. For in March of 1901, after J. Pierpont Morgan had created the United States Steel Corporation, the newspapers — or such of them as had not set out to bask in the sun of Empire, Bigness and Industrial and Imperial Might — were filled with gloomy forebodings of a corporate feudalism, whether beneficent or no. And the other side of the feudal shield was Communism, or so more than one editorial writer thought; Arthur Brisbane, the son of a socialist of Greeley and Brook Farm days, feared, for example, that the epoch of great trusts in the offing would inevitably call forth its counter-principle of a "labor trust more dangerous and aggressive than any other."

Whatever the future might hold, however, the symbolism of United States Steel — fifty per cent Morgan ingenuity, and fifty per cent water — was fairly obvious. It meant the beginning of the end of competition in another basic industry. Previous to March 3, 1901, the Carnegie Steel Company — a vertical trust, controlling its own product from the Lake Superior ore bed to the salesman's order book — had been preëminent in steel; Carnegie had become a byword for ruthless and brilliant competition. The "little Scotch pirate" did not approve of the industrial pools that formed only to break up with the dishonesty of constituent members; he scorned the Morgan "community of interests." His competitors felt this attitude whenever there were hard times — although, for the consumer, the Carnegie tactics were vastly preferable to the methods by which Rockefeller had stabilized the oil industry and, incidentally, obtained control of ninety-five per cent of the product.

Carnegie, in 1900, wanted to retire. For thirty years he had nourished a dream; he wanted to be both Mæcenas to the arts and Lord Bountiful to organized charity. "The man who dies rich," he said, with a touch of the characteristic Carnegie disingenuousness, "dies disgraced." But before a career of ostentatious and fully publicized giving could be undertaken as a diversion for old age, Carnegie must dispose of his steel works. And he wanted them in safe hands.

There was one man in America who could consolidate steel, and he was J. Pierpont Morgan. But Morgan was loath to act, even though Elbert H. Gary had urged upon him the desirability of stabilized steel. He certainly never would have acted at Carnegie's direct invitation for bouncing, twinkling Andy, the "little white-haired Scotch devil" of Tom Scott's affection, was the type of person which the gruff, powerful Morgan could not stomach. Carnegie, however, had guile sufficient to the task. He literally bluffed Morgan into purchasing the Carnegie works and merging them with nine other corporations to form the greatest trust in the world.

Pierpontifex Maximus, as he was known behind his back, had just achieved a fair measure of stability in the railroad world after ten years of work, taking the bankrupt lines of the early nineties and putting them on a relatively non-competitive basis. His National Tube Works, which had bought much of its material from the Carnegie concern, proposed to erect additional blast furnaces and steel works. To Carnegie, this seemed unfriendly. So, in retaliation, the Scotchman threatened to "establish an extensive pipe-and-tube manufacturing plant, representing an investment of $12,000,000," which would have meant a steel war, involving Morgan's interests. But Morgan failed to respond to the retaliatory threat. Carnegie countered by playing his trump card: he circulated the rumor that he was planning his own railroad lines in Pennsylvania to compete with roads under the Morgan domination from Pittsburgh to the seaboard. Morgan became uneasy as stocks began to fluctuate. And then Carnegie, the guileful, sent the man with the tongue of honey, Charles M. Schwab, to New York. Coupled with Schwab's suave representations, the threat of unsettling the railroad situation — which might have entailed a disastrous renewal of the rate-wars of Jay Gould's day — brought Morgan to the bait; he decided to "do something about this fellow Carnegie." The result was the purchase of the Carnegie Steel Company, and the subsequent capitalization of United States Steel at $1,403,450,000. Carnegie was paid off, largely, in bonds; he said he took the total bond issue of the new corporation — $303,450,000 — instead of stocks because the stock was not water alone, but air. Carnegie was right about the water and air, but Morgan's version of the deal also had its truth: he had paid the Scotchman off in bonds, he said, because he wished him forever out of steel in any active way — Morgan had had enough of "Carnegie cattle work along the border."

Carnegie could now achieve his wish to die poor. And consolidation in American industry was relieved of its greatest threat: the Carnegie competitive methods. The consolidation of steel was a culmination, in a way, of a movement that had been going on ever since the Civil War, only to be interrupted periodically by panic, such as that of '93. Trust-forming, which had been outlawed supposedly by the Sherman Act of 1890, had picked up again after the panic of the early nineties by use of the holding-

company device, a method made possible by the wording of the Sherman Law and the easy attitude of New Jersey and Delaware, both of which went into the business of selling industrial indulgences and absolution. By 1898 the United States had ceased to be a "commodity" country, and had become a manufacturing and exporting nation. Cheap raw materials, a plethora of foodstuffs, a constant supply of immigrant labor, the high tariff — made even higher by the Dingley bill of 1897 — and an expanding market — all of these happy factors combined to increase manufactures eleven-fold in value between 1850 and 1900. Population and the value of agricultural products, in the meantime, had increased only three-fold; hence it was not unnatural that the balance of political power had shifted from the rural to the urban districts.

The Spanish-American War had stayed, for a moment, the apprehension of trusts and monopolies, an apprehension that had characterized the late eighties and early nineties. But the consolidation of steel revived the bogey of corporate wealth. And the little fellow, the small business man, the "forgotten man" of that day and generation, if he chose to look at the statistics soon after the new century had opened, might well have feared for his future. In 1899 the Amalgamated Copper Company and the American Smelting and Refining Company had been formed. The American Sugar Refining Company, a trust of the 1891 vintage, had escaped the teeth of the Sherman Act by a fortunate Supreme Court decision which said, in effect, that control of ninety-five per cent of a product did not constitute a monopoly in restraint of trade. The Standard Oil had been reorganized under the Jersey laws in 1899; the Consolidated Tobacco Company was formed in 1901; the International Mercantile Marine in 1902. In 1904, there were, according to John Moody's figures, 318 industrial trusts representing mergers of practically 5,300 plants and a capitalization exceeding seven billions. By 1914 companies doing an annual business ranging from over a hundred thousand to a million dollars, and the class above a million dollars, employed more than three-fourths of the wage earners and made more than four-fifths (in value) of the products of a nation.

The movement toward consolidation had gone on in the railroad world, as well as in the industrial, with the result that, by 1900, nearly all of the high-grade mileage was controlled by six groups: the Vanderbilts (who dominated the New York Central and the Northeast, excepting New England); the Pennsylvania system; the Morgan-Hill combination in the Northwest; the Gould-Rockefeller lines in the far Southwest, with connections to the Atlantic seaboard; the Harriman lines (Union and Southern Pacifics and the Illinois Central); and the Moore group (the Rock Island and other lines leading into Chicago). The Rockefeller and the Morgan interests were heavily invested in the independent New Haven road, and the Vanderbilt and Rockefeller groups had large blocks of stock in the Delaware and Hudson. A "trustification of money," as the Pujo investigation of thirteen years later would reveal, had made all this consolidation possible.

More fundamental to it, in a philosophical sense, was the Great Technology made possible by the development of the scientific method, the Baconian outlook. And even as business consolidation was coming to its flourishing peak, the methods of the Great Technology were making their impact felt in the world of the American magazine, with results that would cause the plutocratic masters of the industrial centralization to shiver — for a brief moment.

In the beginning, however, the genius of the American cheap magazine was Frank A. Munsey, as money-bound a man as any captain of industry or promoter who ever trod the corner at Wall and Broad Streets. This curious country boy from Maine, who chose literature, of all things, as a stepping-stone to wealth, had come into a magazine world that, at the beginning of the nineties, was strangely out of touch with the realities of American life. The magazines were neither published and sold by modern methods, nor were their contents at all in tune with life as the American knew it. Until 1890, the "big four" were the literary magazines — the *Atlantic, Scribner's, Harper's* and the *Century*, which sold at twenty-five to thirty-five cents a copy. *Harper's* was edited by Henry Mills Alden, with George W. Curtis and, later, William Dean Howells, in the Editor's Easy Chair. *Scribner's* was looked after by Edward L. Burlingame, who made it an illustrated literary magazine, like *Harper's*, but with more attention paid to art and to the special department of wood engraving. The *Century*, under Richard Watson Gilder, was, perhaps, even more "literary" than *Scribner's* or *Harper's*. The *Atlantic Monthly*, which had published Lloyd's attack on the Standard Oil and the rebate system, had more diversity of appeal than the three others, and was edited by greater men, commencing with James Russell Lowell and continuing through the tenure of William Dean Howells. But, one and all, they were citadels of the "genteel tradition," survivors out of the world of the scholar gentleman.

Into this tepid arena, at the beginning of the nineties, plunged Frank A. Munsey, with his belief in Ford methods — "big volume and small margins." Munsey was to the modern magazine, in America, what E. W. Scripps was to the newspaper: the father of literary mass production. Innovations in the printing art had made a cheap magazine possible by 1891, the year of the founding of Munsey's in its twenty-five-cent incarnation. Glazed paper made from woodpulp — a cheaper medium than ragpaper — and the invention of the photoengraving process had combined to reduce the mechanical costs. American advertising was already on the rise. But the wholesalers — consisting of the American News Company of New York, with its forty or fifty branches throughout the country — stood, a monopoly, in the way of the pioneer.

Before Munsey's adventure, S. S. McClure had launched his McClure's at fifteen cents in 1893. John Brisben Walker, who had founded the Cosmopolitan in 1886, cut his magazine to twelve-and-one-half cents a copy, but was soon back to fifteen. But it is doubtful if either of these competitors would have been able to maintain their fifteen-cent front if Munsey had not come along, in 1893, with a ten-cent magazine, the first in the country, to dramatize the change.

The middlemen — those who bought, perforce, from the American News Company — refused from the start to handle Munsey's at the stipulated wholesaler's price of seven cents a magazine. And the refusal was almost fatal. Munsey had no printing plant of his own, no electrotyping establishment, no bindery. His capital, as he said, was all on "the wrong side of the ledger." But he held out for the seven-cent price. A vicious trade war resulted, and Munsey, oddly enough for a timid man, won the scrap; by 1899, his investment was worth $5,000,000, his monthly circulation had reached 650,000. With his Down-East shrewdness, the triumphant editor — in an article called "The Making and Marketing of Munsey's Magazine," published in Munsey's for December, 1899 — pointed out that articles, fiction, engraving and pictures cost no more for an edition of a million copies than for one of a thousand.

Munsey's admiration was not for the quality of his articles, fiction, engraving and pictures, most of which were of a low grade; his praise was all for bigness. "If all the paper used in these four [Munsey] magazines every month," he wrote, "were made into a ribbon as wide as the magazine itself, it would cover a distance of 22,916 miles, or go nearly around the world." Or if it were made into "the ticker in a stockbroker's office, it would cover 366,644 miles, or go around the world nearly fifteen times." There speaks the authentic voice of the Boy Broker.

But a better man than Munsey was in the field made safe by the survival of a ten-cent magazine; he was S. S. McClure, the greatest magazine genius America has produced, an Antrim Irishman, blond, ebullient, enthusiastic, forever on the wing, seeking ideas and authors to carry them out, the man who brought Kipling's Kim to America and who became, himself, a character in two novels, Robert Louis Stevenson's The Wrecker and Howells's A Hazard of New Fortunes. During the nineties the superior caliber of McClure was not immediately apparent. As the new century opened, however, McClure was feeling his way toward a dynamic social conception of the uses of a cheap magazine. The biggest fact of American life was — the business consolidation. McClure knew it in his bones. He had sent some one to the Armour Institute of Technology, which had been established in Chicago at the time of the World's Fair, to write it up, and the author had included in his article some material about Mr. Armour and the packing industry. This gave McClure a lead: he decided to have articles written definitely about the most important American businesses. It was suggested in the McClure offices that the methods of handling and distribution of the Standard Oil Company would be of interest, so McClure planned a series on oil to begin in February of 1897. The talk about trusts, started by Henry Demarest Lloyd, had become general, McClure noted, but he had no bias either for or against them at the time.

There happened to be, on the *McClure's* staff, a motherly young woman who had once taught Sunday school in Frederic C. Howe's home in the oil regions of Northwestern Pennsylvania — Miss Ida M. Tarbell. She had already demonstrated her ability at historical research in the period of the French Revolution, and had recently written a popular life of Lincoln. McClure put her on the job of looking into the Standard Oil — a job that was to take five years of study before she had completely mastered and checked up on all the material for the famous *History of the Standard Oil Company*. Three years of research were put in before the first chapter was printed in *McClure's* for November of 1902.

This was hardly muck-raking in cold blood, however. Miss Tarbell, who was credited, later, whether slanderously or not, with having an animus against the Rockefellers because of the ruin of her own relatives in the early years of the oil business, merely saw with the logic of her background the little fellow as the

noble fellow; the Standard Oil, through no preconceived plan in McClure's mind, became, again, the "Anaconda, hideous in his deformity," as it had been in Lloyd's *Wealth Against Commonwealth*. But events conspired to make one series of haphazardly muck-raking articles the beginning of a campaign.

The business consolidation that stared McClure in the face at the end of the nineties had not been attained by wholly extra-political means. An invisible government had passed over the country coextensive and coeval with its westward expansion. Laws were enacted in the interests of business. As William Allen White humorously remarked: "It was just as easy to see the railroad's side as it was to see the other side, so the mass of Federal decisions for years favored the railroads." And the railroads were the foundation of the structure. The wholly legal "corruption" of the courts — we may assume that no money was passed — was merely the capstone of what Lincoln Steffens, McClure's greatest muckraker, was shortly to baptize "the System."

Out in Cleveland, as Ida Tarbell's first article was about to appear, Tom L. Johnson was already fighting a System that had corrupted the city government in the interests of maintaining a traction monopoly, keeping carfares up, and paying a high dividend upon heavily watered stock. Miss Tarbell suggested to McClure that an article on certain admirable aspects of the city government of Cleveland would be worth while. A "constructive" person, Miss Tarbell. So Steffens, who had just joined Ray Stannard Baker and Miss Tarbell on the McClure staff, went West with no definite idea in mind, but with a hazy notion that copy, either by himself or others, awaited him. While on his trip some one old him of corruption in St. Louis, where certain Joseph W. Folk, circuit attorney, was fighting a ring of boodlers. The result was, after some investigation, a joint article in *McClure's* for October, 1902, written by Claude H. Wetmore, a St. Louis reporter, and Steffens himself, called "Tweed Days in St. Louis." It was the first muckrake article — having beaten Ida Tarbell's first piece on the Standard Oil to the newsstands by a month. Thus was S. S. McClure involved in muck-raking.

And then came the yelping of the muck-rake pack. The dogs let loose, they swarmed all over the land, doing some harm, but an incalculable amount of good in the way of educating the American people to realities. Muck-raking, indeed, provided the basis for the entire movement toward Social Democracy that came to its head in the first Wilson Administration. This movement, it is true, grew out of Populism, and was aided by the spread of socialism, but it never would have gone very far without the incessant din in the American cheap magazines during the Roosevelt and Taft administrations. McClure, having genius, shaped it at the start into educational channels. He had always had a passion for education, and the muckraking he undertook to foster was always documented, sane, "proved" to the last fact. And he was thorough; not one article would he have on an aspect of the growth of American industrialism, with its political concomitants, but would grow into a series, exposing the anatomy entire. An Englishman, William Archer, comparing the flaccid cheap magazine of London with our own, was moved to remark that "the historian of the future may determine how much of the 'uplift' that distinguished the Roosevelt Administration was due to the influence of the McClure type of magazine; we cannot, at this distance of time, see things quite in proportion; but it seems to me certain that Mr. McClure both paved the way for President Roosevelt and potently furthered the movement with which his name will always be identified."

The yelps of the pack grew louder, bolder. The *History of the Standard Oil Company* continued on through 1903. Steffens, excited by what he had found in St. Louis, pursued corruption to Minneapolis, to Cleveland, to Cincinnati, to Chicago, to Philadelphia, to New York — writing a series that grew into a handbook of American city government as it was at the beginning of the century and, indeed, is to-day. Steffens's articles were later gathered into a book, *The Shame of the Cities*. A second series on the shame of the States — called *Enemies of the Republic* in *McClure's* and *The Struggle for Self-Government* in book form — followed from Steffens's pen. Ray Stannard Baker commenced to explore the labor problem, finding graft even in labor organizations, but more duplicity among the employers. *Everybody's Magazine* picked up the challenge, commencing with Thomas W. Lawson's *Frenzied Finance* (1905), and printing Charles Edward Russell's exposures of the beef trust in the same year. Samuel Hopkins Adams investigated the patent-medicine situation — or racket, as we would call it to-day — in *Collier's*, spreading some horrible stories throughout 1905. And in the same year Ray Stannard Baker, in *McClure's*, started *The Railroads on Trial*, a series that would run on into 1906, when the debates in Congress were leading up to the Hepburn Rate Bill, which would put at least one or two teeth into the Interstate Commerce Commission.

Other notable additions to the "literature of protest" there were, too. Burton

J. Hendrick told the story of Life Insurance in 1906 to a *McClure's* audience that had been very much excited by the insurance investigation conducted by Charles Evans Hughes in 1905. David Graham Phillips, the reporter and novelist, wrote a blistering, peppery, and sometimes inaccurate series called "The Treason of the Senate" for the *Cosmopolitan* in 1906. His facts were assembled for him by Gustavus Myers, according to Isaac Marcosson, but it is questionable that he used them as Myers himself would have used them. The *Cosmopolitan* having been bought by Hearst, it commenced, with Phillips's articles to give muck-raking the tone of the yellow journals. But Phillips's series was, in the main, justified, as Steffens's work was already there to prove. The campaign went on, following McClure's lead, on the one hand, and Hearst's on the other. Russell traced the connection in California between the Southern Pacific (*The Octopus*) and the State government for *Hampton's* in 1910, the very year that Hiram Johnson, Republican nominee for Governor, decided that the railroad "must be kicked out of politics." Judge Ben Lindsey of the Denver Children's Court wrote on criminal law and juvenile delinquency for *Everybody's* in 1909, with Larry Ritchie, now Hoover's Man Friday, doing some of the investigations for the series. And *McClure's*, seeking to discover the connection between the "System" and prostitution, carried a number of articles by George Kibbe Turner on the "social evil" and allied vice in 1909. The underworld came in for a lurid series by Alfred Henry Lewis, called "The Apaches of New York," which rocketed through *Pearson's Magazine* in 1911–12. Even the *Saturday Evening Post,* in these years, had some of the stigmata of the muck-raking magazine. . . .

Lincoln Steffens was the first to supply the people of the Rooseveltian decade with protective knowledge. The textbooks on American government were woefully deficient in teaching home truths to students of American government, municipal, state and national, and not even James Bryce suspected the worst. "Where," asked William Allen White, the Kansas editor with practical political experience, in a review of *The Shame of the Cities,* "where in the constitution are the functions of the boss described? Where in the constitution are the relations between the local corporation attorney and the people described? Where in the constitution does the chairman of the State Central Committee of the dominant party get his authority to sell legislative indulgences to corporations that contribute to his campaign fund? Where in the constitution may one find how the thing we call capital gets into government at all?"

Steffens gave factual answers to White's rhetorical, though pertinent, list of the Constitution's deficiencies. There is no need to detail the facts here; there is need to sketch the whole picture, the anatomy of municipal, state and national government as Steffens uncovered it. "'Big business,'" he discovered, "was and still is, the current name of the devil, the root of all evil, political and economic." But "'Big Business' . . . is a blind phrase, useless; it leads nowhere." It is true that, in back of political corruption were the railroads, banks, public service corporations, and so on, all of whom stayed in politics, after they had got what they wanted, merely to protect the water in their stocks, so that they might earn the more on the actual investment without raising a hue and cry among the populace. The railroads and public service corporations were, of course, "big," but there were, too, saloons, gambling and bawdy houses, which were small. Even as Henry George had discovered, Steffens learned that what these big and little businesses had in common was not size, but the need of privileges — what La Follette came to call "Special Privilege." They needed franchises and special legislation, which required legislative corruption; they needed protective tariffs and interpretations of the law in their own interests; they needed "pull" with judges, prosecutors and the police.

Privilege, then, was the root of all the evil — to "throw the rascals out" and to put into office "good" men merely caused the "good" men to do "bad" things, for "privilege" still remained — the "good" men had to choose between parties clamoring for this "privilege." The very act of choice connoted "pressure" and "corruption" in some one's eyes. Society, said Steffens, was paradoxical in its system of rewards and punishments. It taught the ideal of success, set up the temptation of power and riches to men and nations, and then *punished the losers*, letting the winners in the race, the successful, the rich, go. "What we ought to do," Steffens concluded, "is to let the losers of the race go, and take down the prizes we offer to the winners."

While Steffens was uncovering "political corruption" — which is, as he proved, merely a hypocritical and long-winded phrase for "politics" — Ida Tarbell was showing that business was "bad" in itself; that, to succeed, a business man had to eat up, crush, scotch, trample out his rival for materials, credit and markets. And Ray Stannard Baker was describing the corruption of labor unions by contractors in the building business who, in turn, got their jobs and opportunities through political pressure. In a notable article, published in *McClure's* for September, 1903, Baker demonstrated how "Capital and Labor Hunt Together" in Chicago, whose citizens were made the victims "of the new industrial conspiracy." This article does much to clear up the question of how far back in Chicago life the racketeer's pedigree goes; "Al" Capone, it shows, is merely one human milestone along an old, old road.

On investigation, Baker discovered a merger of the interests of the Chicago Coal Teamsters' Union and the Coal Team Owners' Association. Together they had monopolized the coal business of the city. Independent operators, men who owned their own teams and wagons and oftentimes the coal, had banded together, and gone to the Teamsters' Union. "We will," they said, offering an olive branch, "hire no scabs if you, in turn, will haul no coal for outsiders." Labor accepted the terms. "This sort of monopoly," Baker wrote, "is new to our American life" — after "cracking each other," the forces of capital and labor were getting together to crack the public, keeping prices and wages up together. And when natural gas offered competition, the monopoly took care of that by refusing to haul any more coal to Marshall Field and Company, to the Auditorium Hotel, and so on, until an agreement had been signed by the consumers to use no more natural gas for five years.

The coal combination, Baker found, was but one among many — others being The Milk Dealers' Association working hand in glove with the Milk Drivers' Union, and the Sheet Metal Contractors' Association teaming up with the Amalgamated Sheet Metal Workers' Union. Whenever "peaceful" threats failed, these capital-labor combinations in restraint of trade resorted to terrorization — sluggers were brought in, and even murder resulted. It was here that the gangster as an adjunct to business, as a force for "stabilization," got his real start.

In New York, whither Baker pursued his inquiries, the startling discovery was made that the building trades were using the labor boss as their new tool, and a situation similar to that in Chicago had developed. In San Francisco, labor grew so strong, after 1901, that it owned the town. The labor unions elected their own mayor, got a grip on the city, and drove the scab out. Then followed a labor monopoly of business — with the capitalists taken into partnership. Working on the Chicago principle, wages were put up twenty-five per cent, and prices from fifty to one hundred per cent. The distance of San Francisco from the Eastern labor market made all this possible.

Baker went on from his labor explorations, which included a study of the Western Federation of Miners, most militant, idealistic and disciplined of labor organizations, to a comprehensive report of the iniquity of the railroads — with particular emphasis on the rebate evil, forced by the Standard Oil seeking a favorable rate on refined oil, by the Carnegie Steel Company, by the beef trust and by the fruit industry. "Control the rate, and you control the railroad," was his formulation of the reason for the rebate. Chicago packers, he found, underpaid the cattle raisers, and overcharged the meat consumers, by means of the trust which had been built up on the rebate. The packers, he wrote, were "traitors to the principles of democracy." The methods of the beef trust of Armour, Swift and the rest — suddenly dramatized for the country in 1906 by the appearance of Upton Sinclair's *The Jungle* — were documented by Charles Edward Russell, in his *The Greatest Trust in the World*, which was serialized in *Everybody's* in 1905. "The men who operate [this trust]" said Russell, with the extenuation of the nascent socialist, "are very good men" as the world goes, but are

caught by the system and "driven along by an economic evolution beyond their knowledge or control."

The picture of society painted by the muck-rakers was amazingly complete although the fiction purveyed by Mc Clure and other editors of the time was feeble, dilatory and false to the life in the surrounding articles. But realism in fiction would come later. McClure himself was not content to halt at money corruption — his complaint with Steffen was that *The Shame of the Cities* and *Enemies of the Republic* stopped short with the financial aspects. And so, when McClure was informed by the Boston *Evening Transcript* that Americans were a moral people, and lived just as well under corrupt government as not, he set out to determine the truth of this ukase. The *Transcript* was routed by the fact McClure turned up. Taking the period of our most rapid expansion, McClure found that in the years between 188 and 1895 murder in the United States had increased six times as rapidly as the population, and was thirty times as frequent per million inhabitants as in the countries of Northern Europe. George Kibbe Turner, an addition to the *Mc Clure* staff, was turned loose on Chicago to uncover the human waste that was the concomitant of the System which Steffen had portrayed in terms of the waste of dollars and cents. Turner's article on the relation between municipal government and the exploitation of women led to famous Vice Commission's Report of Chicago, and Archer, the English critic of the muck-raking magazines, was duly impressed with the "amazing picture of organized, police-protected vice and crime — a picture every line of which was evidently the result of patient, penetrating investigation and intimate personal knowledge."

Others were not moved by the Olym

pian patience of the notable staff of *Mc-Clure's*. Sensationalism, the raucous note, the blood-hound bell, the combined methods of the stock promoter and the yellow journalist, entered the muck-rake arena with the publication by *Everybody's* of *Frenzied Finance*, by Thomas W. Lawson of Boston. Taking over Lincoln Steffens's phrase, "the System," Lawson, a stock-market operator of the most flagrant gambling stripe, applied it to the methods of Big Business, the bankers and the State Street and Wall Street brokers. Lawson was used to the grand manner — or the gambler's simulation of the grand manner. He dedicated his story — the "inside" story of the Amalgamated Copper Company — with a rhetorical flourish to "Penitence and Punishment," but it was plain, from both his past and later behavior, that neither penitence nor punishment concerned this ebullient soul. Lawson's very method of getting his series before the public smacked of his methods as the President of Trinity Copper — he was the "promoter" in literature, even as he was the promoter in stock-rigging and the advertisement of his curious estate at "Dreamwold." *Everybody's*, at the time, was an obscure magazine, not yet one of the ornaments of the literature of protest. To its owners Lawson came, asking no recompense for his series, but demanding only that the magazine spend $50,000 or more in advertising his financial peepshow. By his own account, Lawson added $250,000 more for publicity purposes, and the circulation of *Everybody's* responded at once, mounting, within a year, from 150,000 to more than 750,000. Crowds jostled and clamored each month for the latest installment of the series. "The System," as explained by Lawson, "is a process or a device for the incubation of wealth from the people's savings in the banks, trust and insurance compa-

nies, and the public funds." Lawson's characterizations of the beneficiaries of "the System" — of J. E. O. Addicks of Delaware, of Widener and Elkins of Philadelphia and public utilities fame, of H. H. Rogers and William Rockefeller of the Standard Oil, of James Stillman of the National City Bank, of F. Augustus Heinze, copper man of Montana, and of James R. Keene, the horse-racing broker whom Morgan had used to "make a market" for the newly incorporated United States Steel — all these were vivid, touched with the malice that makes for edge. As such, they made ridiculous Lawson's protest that he took no issue with men; "it is with a principle I am concerned."

The story of the Amalgamated was the story of racketeering in copper stocks, of foisting large quantities of water upon an always gullible public. There was truth, plenty of it, in what Lawson had to tell, as *Barron's* published journals were later to reveal, but Lawson's singular concern for the moral fiber of the community was unconvincing; and the skepticism of the newspapers was borne out, in 1908, when Lawson, disgusted, as he said, with the "saffron-blooded apes" of the public, went back to his first love, stock speculation.

Even as the methods of frenzied financiers were under process of exposure in the pages of *Everybody's*, the literature of protest, of exposure, was not yet known as "muck-raking." The first mistake, the signal that the top of the movement had been reached and deterioration had set in, was yet to be made; but it was not long in coming. William Randolph Hearst, it was, who made the slip — who brought odium upon the muckrakers, all of them, whether good or bad. While the Hepburn Railway Rate Bill was being debated in a recalcitrant Senate, with a public fed upon Ray Stannard

Baker's *The Railroads on Trial* watching
the fate of the legislation with eager
eyes, Hearst announced that his *Cosmopolitan* would initiate a number of exposures that would be "the most vascular
and virile" thus far printed. The Hearst
bill of particulars contained a sneer at
McClure's and its staff — "well-meaning
and amazingly industrious persons writing without inspiration" who had succeeded only in piling up "indiscriminate
masses of arid facts."

What Hearst had in mind, for the *Cosmopolitan*, was a series of articles called
"The Treason of the Senate," by David
Graham Phillips, a former Pulitzer em-
ployee and a novelist of some repute.
This was a logical move, since the Senate, next to the Supreme Court, was the
most important cog in the machinery of
the "politics of acquisition and enjoyment." Phillips, however, was not the
best man in the world for the job —
Steffens, who had written on "the boss
of the Senate," Nelson Aldrich of Rhode
Island, would have turned out far more
reliable stuff. But Steffens, of course, was
a dealer in "arid facts," trained by Godkin of the *Post*, not Pulitzer of the *World;*
while Phillips, on the other hand, had a
vigorous supply of the best Hearstian
epithets. His series commenced in the
March issue of the *Cosmopolitan* and
continued for nine months — running
under the epigraph from the Constitution: "Treason against the United States
shall consist only in levying war against
them, or in adhering to their enemies,
giving them aid and comfort." "The
Senate," he wrote, "is the eager, resource-
ful, indefatigable agent of interests as
hostile to the American people as any
invading army could be, and vastly more
dangerous: interests that manipulate the
prosperity produced by all, so that it
heaps up riches for the few; interests

whose growth and power can only mean
the degradation of the people, of the
educated into sycophants, of the masses
toward serfdom."

Corruption being the attempt to serve
two opposed masters, the Senators, Phillips said, came within the definition of
the word. They were elected by the
people, whom they nominally represented, but they served the "interests."
The first to be brought upon the carpet
by Phillips was Chauncey Mitchell Depew, the "Vanderbilt-New York Central"
Senator. Then followed the chastise-
ments of Aldrich of Rhode Island, whose
daughter had become the wife of John
D. Rockefeller, Jr., and whose very good
friend was J. Pierpont Morgan. Aldrich,
a Hamiltonian with expensive tastes, was
the "right arm of the 'interests'"; Arthur
Pue Gorman, Democrat of Maryland,
was the "left." Other members of the
"merger" of Democrats and Republicans
for betraying the people to the "interests"
were Spooner of Wisconsin, Bailey of
Texas, Elkins of West Virginia, "Fire
Alarm" Foraker of Ohio, stipendiary of
the Standard Oil, Lodge of Massachu-
setts, "the familiar coarse type of machine politician, disguised by the robes
of the 'Gentleman Scholar,'" Allison of
Iowa, master of compromise and Aldrich's chief spreader of salve, and so on.

The series stirred much interest, and
brought forth a general reviling of Phillips from the ranks of the unco' guid,
although men there were to back up the
charge that the United States Senate had
become the "Rich Man's Club" and the
American "House of Lords." Phillips was
embittered by the attacks, and refused
to write any more articles, but, a
Charles Edward Russell wrote to Cornelius C. Regier of the University of
Iowa (author of an excellent unpub-
lished thesis on "The Era of Muck-

rakers"), "in two years . . . it was a common remark that he had purified the Senate."

It was the thoroughly justified attack on "poor old Chauncey Depew" that constituted the slip which brought the term "muck-raker" upon the *littérateurs* of exposure, and it was Theodore Roosevelt, who thought Norris's *The Octopus* and Sinclair's *The Jungle* overdrawn, who was responsible for tarring the whole school—from Ray Stannard Baker and Lincoln Steffens, the scholars of the movement, to Phillips and Lawson, the dealers in pyrotechnics. At a private dinner of the Gridiron Club, on March 17, 1906, Roosevelt took as his text a passage from Bunyan's *Pilgrim's Progress* ". . . the Man with the Muckrake, the man who could look no way but downward with the muckrake in his hand; who was offered a celestial crown for his muckrake but who would neither look up nor regard the crown he was offered but continued to rake to himself the filth of the floor." The speech was not reported, for it is the Gridiron Club's rule to preserve strict privacy of expressed opinion, but gossip of the characterization spread nonetheless. So Roosevelt, with his instinctive recognition of the moment to strike, decided to get the speech "reported in full." At an engagement which he had to dedicate the cornerstone of the House of Representatives Office Building, on April 14, 1906, he balanced an attack on Big Business with an attack on the "lunatic fringe" of the magazine writers. The fact that it was aimed only at the lunatic fringe was, however, quickly forgotten. The word "muck-raker" was seized upon by a public that had acquired a taste for the Roosevelt epithets. The President had forever fixed a name to a generation, a decade, a school of writers. Whatever

T. R.'s sins may have been (and we shall come to them), he at least had the virtue of picturesque and salty speech. Steffens, Tarbell and Baker, Phillips, Lawson and Russell — they had to like the term, for it would follow them for the rest of their lives.

After Roosevelt's denunciation, muckraking trickled out. Charles Edward Russell, one of the most earnest men who ever wrote a paragraph, accepted the designation blithely, and continued to expose rottenness wherever he found it. In 1912 he was still hammering away at the railroads, at special privilege. But he couldn't "go it alone," with no support, so he had joined the Socialist Party. Baker, after helping La Follette write his autobiography, turned to his essays in contentment, which he published under the name of David Grayson. Steffens became interested in a Christian socialism, in the application of the Golden Rule to industry, and in revolutions. Miss Tarbell became a Yes Woman for the Judge Garys and Owen D. Youngs — the critical sense gone. And muck-raking degenerated in style and acumen — done, where it was done, sporadically. The sweeping, documented, balanced surveys which McClure had paid thousands of dollars to assemble gave way to the single article, which shed a little light on one spot, but put no wrong in its historical setting. "Meaning" had gone out of muck-raking.

Why did "The Magazines Soft Pedal"? Russell sought to tell the public in *Pearson's* for February, 1914. It was the advertising departments of magazines that had put a damper on the muckraking spirit. The department stores had easily held two ends of the garrotte around the newspapers' necks, he said, quoting La Follette's argument of 1912, but the magazines were more difficult to subdue. A combination among manufacturers, and bank control, however, led to "undue" influence, and the magazines sold out. *Everybody's*, he said, lost seven pages of advertising in an issue when his series on the beef trust was running — and the advertisements which disappeared were of hams, preserved meats, soap, patent cleansers and fertilizers, and railroads. Whole pages went glimmering when Russell commenced writing about the tobacco trust — which was nominally dissolved by the Supreme Court in Taft's Administration. Mournfully, writing as one in at the death, Russell listed the defunct muck-raking magazines — *Hampton's*, the old *Arena*, *Success*, the *National Post*, *Human Life*, the *Twentieth Century*. *McClure's* became a pretty-pretty magazine, a purveyor of cheap fiction; the *American*, which had been remade by Steffens and Miss Tarbell into a muck-raking organ for a short interlude, turned into its present incarnation. But more potent than the advertiser's garrotte — and the garrotte played its part, we may be sure, whether openly or through the growth of a new "community of interest" in the magazine field — was the indifference of a public that still allowed itself to be destroyed through lack of knowledge; the public that thought the Rooseveltian and Wilsonian reforms were bringing in the millennium, instead of driving the methods of a rapacious industry underground and clearing a path for the new magniloquence of "service."

What did the muck-rakers accomplish? On the theory that it takes a lot of running by the human animal to remain in the same place, a great deal. The Hepburn Act, . . . was one triumph in the muck-rakers' list; the labor legislation of the Wilson terms undoubtedly owed much to the magazine agitation. The direct election of United States Senators may have been aided by Phillips. The pure food laws harked back to Sinclair's *The Jungle*, a muck-rake novel. The Bureau of Corporations, and the anti-trust activities, feeble though they were in promoting competition and preventing monopoly, rested on the work of inquisitive magazine writers who continued the social thinking of the Populists. But the muck-rakers could do nothing to keep down the rising cost of living, which was the most conspicuous phenomenon to the average man in the years just before the War. They could do nothing to iron out the business cycle, which is a more important aspect of life under a machine civilization than all the graft in the world. They could do nothing, ultimately, to right any of the fundamental wrongs — and perhaps the public was wiser than it knew in growing tired of the good old sport of exposing those who "do us good and plenty."

The English critic, William Archer, hit upon the weakness of the muck-rake magazines in 1910. "The logical weakness of their position," he wrote, "lies in an insufficient thinking-out of the fundamental ideas on which their crusade is based. They do not see that most of the evils they attack are inevitable results of the national creed of individualism. They lack either the insight or the courage to admit that some form of collectivism is the only permanent check upon the enslavement of the people by the most amazing plutocracy the world has ever seen." McClure himself, intelligent though he was, could only find a remedy for the ills his reporters had turned up in the commission form of government. I wonder what he would have had to say in 1931 when Cleveland abandoned the city manager plan because it had fallen into the hands of the "old gang," the machine?

V. RECENT REAPPRAISALS OF MUCKRAKING

Lincoln Steffens: SHAME OF THE CITIES

In Shame of the Cities (1904) Lincoln Steffens brought together several of his articles on municipal corruption that originally appeared in McClure's magazine. In the introduction to the book Steffens outlined his approach to the problem. He was particularly concerned that the business spirit pervaded government. He placed responsibility for corruption upon the people but still believed in the essential soundness of the American character.

THIS is not a book. It is a collection of articles reprinted from *McClure's Magazine*. Done as journalism, they are journalism still, and no further pretensions are set up for them in their new dress. This classification may seem pretentious enough; certainly it would if I should confess what claims I make for my profession. But no matter about that; I insist upon the journalism. And there is my justification for separating from the bound volumes of the magazine and republishing, practically without reediting, my accounts as a reporter of the shame of American cities. They were written with a purpose, they were published serially with a purpose, and they are reprinted now together to further that same purpose, which was and is — to sound for the civic pride of an apparently shameless citizenship.

There must be such a thing, we reasoned. All our big boasting could not be empty vanity, nor our pious pretensions hollow sham. American achievements in science, art, and business mean sound abilities at bottom, and our hypocrisy a race sense of fundamental ethics. Even

in government we have given proofs of potential greatness, and our political failures are not complete; they are simply ridiculous. But they are ours. Not alone the triumphs and the statesmen, the defeats and the grafters also represent us, and just as truly. Why not see it so and say it?

Because, I heard, the American people won't "stand for" it. You may blame the politicians, or, indeed, any one class, but not all classes, not the people. Or you may put it on the ignorant foreign immigrant, or any one nationality, but not on all nationalities, not on the American people. But no one class is at fault, nor any one breed, nor any particular interest or group of interests. The misgovernment of the American people is misgovernment by the American people.

When I set out on my travels, an honest New Yorker told me honestly that I would find that the Irish, the Catholic Irish, were at the bottom of it all everywhere. The first city I went to was St. Louis, a German city. The next was Minneapolis, a Scandinavian city, with a leadership of New Englanders. Then

From Lincoln Steffens, *Shame of the Cities* (Doubleday & Company, Inc., 1961), pp. 1–18.

came Pittsburgh, Scotch Presbyterian, and that was what my New York friend was. "Ah, but they are all foreign populations," I heard. The next city was Philadelphia, the purest American community of all, and the most hopeless. And after that came Chicago and New York, both mongrel-bred, but the one a triumph of reform, the other the best example of good government that I had seen. The "foreign element" excuse is one of the hypocritical lies that save us from the clear sight of ourselves.

Another such conceit of our egotism is that which deplores our politics and lauds our business. This is the wail of the typical American citizen. Now, the typical American citizen is the business man. The typical business man is a bad citizen; he is busy. If he is a "big business man" and very busy, he does not neglect, he is busy with politics, oh, very busy and very businesslike. I found him buying boodlers in St. Louis, defending grafters in Minneapolis, originating corruption in Pittsburgh, sharing with bosses in Philadelphia, deploring reform in Chicago, and beating good government with corruption funds in New York. He is a self-righteous fraud, this big business man. He is the chief source of corruption, and it were a boon if he would neglect politics. But he is not the business man that neglects politics; that worthy is the good citizen, the typical business man. He too is busy, he is the one that has no use and therefore no time for politics. When his neglect has permitted bad government to go so far that he can be stirred to action, he is unhappy, and he looks around for a cure that shall be quick, so that he may hurry back to the shop. Naturally, too, when he talks politics, he talks shop. His patent remedy is quack; it is business.

"Give us a business man," he says ("like me," he means). "Let him introduce business methods into politics and government; then I shall be left alone to attend to my business."

There is hardly an office from United States Senator down to Alderman in any part of the country to which the business man has not been elected; yet politics remains corrupt, government pretty bad, and the selfish citizen has to hold himself in readiness like the old volunteer firemen to rush forth at any hour, in any weather, to prevent the fire; and he goes out sometimes and he puts out the fire (after the damage is done) and he goes back to the shop sighing for the business man in politics. The business man has failed in politics as he has in citizenship. Why?

Because politics is business. That's what's the matter with it. That's what's the matter with everything — art, literature, religion, journalism, law, medicine — they're all business, and all — as you see them. Make politics a sport, as they do in England, or a profession, as they do in Germany, and we'll have — well, something else than we have now — if we want it, which is another question. But don't try to reform politics with the banker, the lawyer, and the dry-goods merchant, for these are business men and there are two great hindrances to their achievement of reform: one is that they are different from, but no better than, the politicians; the other is that politics is not "their line." There are exceptions both ways. Many politicians have gone out into business and done well (Tammany ex-mayors, and nearly all the old bosses of Philadelphia are prominent financiers in their cities), and business men have gone into politics and done well (Mark Hanna, for example). They haven't reformed their adopted trades, however, though they have sometimes sharpened them most pointedly. The politician is a business man with a specialty. When a business man of some other line learns the business of politics, he is a politician, and there is not much reform left in him. Consider the United States Senate, and believe me.

The commercial spirit is the spirit of profit, not patriotism; of credit, not honor; of individual gain, not national prosperity; of trade and dickering, not principle. "My business is sacred," says the business man in his heart. "Whatever prospers my business, is good; it must be. Whatever hinders it, is wrong; it must be. A bribe is bad, that is, it is a bad thing to take; but it is not so bad to give one, not if it is necessary to my business." "Business is business" is not a political sentiment, but our politician has caught it. He takes essentially the same view of the bribe, only he saves his self-respect by piling all his contempt upon the bribe-giver, and he has the great advantage of candor. "It is wrong, maybe," he says, "but if a rich merchant can afford to do business with me for the sake of a convenience or to increase his already great wealth, I can afford, for the sake of a living, to meet him half way. I make no pretensions to virtue, not even on Sunday." And as for giving bad government or good, how about the merchant who gives bad goods or good goods, according to the demand?

But there is hope, not alone despair, in the commercialism of our politics. If our political leaders are to be always a lot of political merchants, they will supply any demand we may create. All we have to do is to establish a steady demand for good government. The bosses have us split up into parties. To him parties are nothing but means to his corrupt ends. He "bolts" his party, but we must not; the bribe-giver changes his party, from one election to another, from one county to another, from one city to another, but the honest voter must not. Why? Because if the honest voter cared no more for his party than the politician and the grafter, then the honest vote would govern, and that would be bad — for graft. It is idiotic, this devotion to a machine that is used to take our sovereignty from us. If we would leave parties to the politicians, and would vote not for the party, not even for men, but for the city, and the State, and the nation, we should rule parties, and cities, and States, and nation. If we would vote in mass on the more promising ticket, or, if the two are equally bad, would throw out the party that is in, and wait till the next election and then throw out the other party that is in — then, I say, the commercial politician would feel a demand for good government and he would supply it. That process would take a generation or more to complete, for the politicians now really do not know what good government is. But it has taken as long to develop bad government, and the politicians know what that is. If it would not "go," they would offer something else, and, if the demand were steady, they, being so commercial, would "deliver the goods."

But do the people want good government? Tammany says they don't. Are the people honest? Are the people better than Tammany? Are they better than the merchant and the politician? Isn't our corrupt government, after all, representative?

President Roosevelt has been sneered at for going about the country preaching, as a cure for our American evils, good conduct in the individual, simple honesty, courage, and efficiency. "Platitudes!" the sophisticated say. Platitudes? If my observations have been true, the literal adoption of Mr. Roosevelt's reform scheme would result in a revolution, more radical and terrible to existing institutions, from the Congress to the Church, from the bank to the ward organization, than socialism or even than anarchy. Why, that would change all of us — not alone our neighbors, not alone the grafters, but you and me.

No, the contemned methods of our despised politics are the master methods of our braggart business, and the corruption that shocks us in public affairs we practice ourselves in our private concerns. There is no essential difference between the pull that gets your wife into society or for your book a favorable review, and that which gets a heeler into office, a thief out of jail, and a rich man's son on the board of directors of a corporation; none between the corruption of a labor union, a bank, and a political machine; none between a dummy director of a trust and the caucus-bound member of a legislature; none between a labor boss like Sam Parks, a boss of banks like John D. Rockefeller, a boss of railroads like J. P. Morgan, and a political boss like Matthew S. Quay. The boss is not a political, he is an American institution, the product of a freed people that have not the spirit to be free.

And it's all a moral weakness; a weakness right where we think we are strongest. Oh, we are good — on Sunday, and we are "fearfully patriotic" on the Fourth of July. But the bribe we pay to the janitor to prefer our interests to the landlord's, is the little brother of the bribe passed to the alderman to sell a city street, and the father of the air-brake stock assigned to the president of a railroad to have this life-saving invention adopted on his road. And as for graft, railroad passes, saloon and bawdy-house blackmail, and watered stock, all these

belong to the same family. We are pathetically proud of our democratic institutions and our republican form of government, of our grand Constitution and our just laws. We are a free and sovereign people, we govern ourselves and the government is ours. But that is the point. We are responsible, not our leaders, since we follow them. We *let* them divert our loyalty from the United States to some "party"; we *let* them boss the party and turn our municipal democracies into autocracies and our republican nation into a plutocracy. We cheat our government and we let our leaders loot it, and we let them wheedle and bribe our sovereignty from us. True, they pass for us strict laws, but we are content to let them pass also bad laws, giving away public property in exchange; and our good, and often impossible, laws we allow to be used for oppression and blackmail. And what can we say? We break our own laws and rob our own government, the lady at the custom-house, the lyncher with his rope, and the captain of industry with his bribe and his rebate. The spirit of graft and of lawlessness is the American spirit.

And this shall not be said? Not plainly? William Travers Jerome, the fearless District Attorney of New York, says, "You can say anything you think to the American people. If you are honest with yourself you may be honest with them, and they will forgive not only your candor, but your mistakes." This is the opinion, and the experience too, of an honest man and a hopeful democrat. Who says the other things? Who says "Hush," and "What's the use?" and "ALL's well," when all is rotten? It is the grafter; the coward, too, but the grafter inspires the coward. The doctrine of "addition, division, and silence" is the doctrine of graft. "Don't hurt the party," "Spare the fair fame of the city," are boodle yells. The Fourth of July oration is the "front" of graft. There is no patriotism in it, but treason. It is part of the game. The grafters call for cheers for the flag, "prosperity," and "the party," just as a highway man commands "hands up," and while we are waving and shouting, they float the flag from the nation to the party, turn both into graft factories, and prosperity into a speculative boom to make "weak hands," as the Wall Street phrase has it, hold the watered stock while the strong hands keep the property. "Blame us, blame anybody, but praise the people," this, the politician's advice, is not the counsel of respect for the people, but of contempt. By just such palavering as courtiers play upon the degenerate intellects of weak kings, the bosses, political, financial, and industrial, are befuddling and befooling our sovereign American citizenship; and — likewise — they are corrupting it.

And it is corruptible, this citizenship. "I know what Parks is doing," said a New York union workman, "but what do I care. He has raised my wages. Let him have his graft!" And the Philadelphia merchant says the same thing: "The party leaders may be getting more than they should out of the city, but that doesn't hurt me. It may raise taxes a little, but I can stand that. The party keeps up the protective tariff. If that were cut down, my business would be ruined. So long as the party stands pat on that, I stand pat on the party."

The people are not innocent. That is the only "news" in all the journalism of these articles, and no doubt that was not new to many observers. It was to me. When I set out to describe the corrupt systems of certain typical cities, I meant to show simply how the people were deceived and betrayed. But in the very first study — St. Louis — the startling truth lay bare that corruption was not merely political; it was financial, commercial, social; the ramifications of boodle were so complex, various, and far-reaching, that one mind could hardly grasp them, and not even Joseph W. Folk, the tireless prosecutor, could follow them all. This state of things was indicated in the first article which Claude H. Wetmore and I compiled together, but it was not shown plainly enough. Mr. Wetmore lived in St. Louis, and he had respect for names which meant little to me. But when I went next to Minneapolis alone, I could see more independently, without respect for persons, and there were traces of the same phenomenon. The first St. Louis article was called "Tweed Days in St. Louis," and though the "better citizen" received attention the Tweeds were the center of interest. In "The Shame of Minneapolis," the truth was put into the title; it was the Shame of Minneapolis; not of the Ames administration, not of the Tweeds, but of the city and its citizens. And yet Minneapolis was not nearly so bad as St. Louis; police graft is never so universal as boodle. It is more shocking, but it is so filthy that it cannot involve so large a part of society. So I returned to St. Louis, and I went over the whole ground again, with the people in mind, not alone the caught and convicted boodlers. And this time the true meaning of "Tweed Days in St. Louis" was made plain. The article was called "The Shamelessness of St. Louis," and that was the burden of the story. In Pittsburgh also the people was the subject, and though the civic spirit there was better, the extent of the corruption throughout the social organization of the community was indicated. But it was not till I got to Philadelphia that the possibilities of popular corruption were worked out to the limit of humiliating confession. That was the place for such a study. There is nothing like it in the country, except possibly, in Cincinnati. Philadelphia certainly is not merely corrupt, but corrupted, and this was made clear. Philadelphia was charged up to — the American citizen.

It was impossible in the space of a magazine article to cover in any one city all the phases of municipal government, so I chose cities that typified most strikingly some particular phase or phases. Thus as St. Louis exemplified boodle; Minneapolis, police graft; Pittsburgh, a political and industrial machine; and Philadelphia, general civic corruption; so Chicago was an illustration of reform, and New York of good government. All these things occur in most of these places. There are, and long have been, reformers in St. Louis, and there is to-day police graft there. Minneapolis has bad boodling and council reform, and boodling is breaking out there again. Pittsburgh has general corruption, and Philadelphia a very perfect political machine. Chicago has police graft and a low order of administrative and general corruption which permeates business, labor, and society generally. As for New York, the metropolis might exemplify almost anything that occurs anywhere in American cities, but no city has had for many years such a good administration as was that of Mayor Seth Low.

That which I have made each city stand for, is that which it had most highly developed. It would be absurd to seek for organized reform in St. Louis, for example, with Chicago next door; or for graft in Chicago with Minneapolis so near. After Minneapolis, a description of administrative corruption in Chicago would have seemed like a repetition. Perhaps it was not just to treat only the conspicuous element in each situation. But why should I be just? I was not judging; I arrogated to myself no such function. I was not writing about Chicago for Chicago, but for the other cities, so I picked out what light each had for the instruction of the others. But, if I was never complete, I never exaggerated. Every one of those articles was an understatement, especially where the conditions were bad, and the proof thereof is that while each article seemed to astonish other cities, it disappointed the city which was its subject. Thus my friends in Philadelphia, who knew what there was to know, and those especially who knew what I knew, expressed surprise that I reported so little. And one St. Louis newspaper said that "the facts were thrown at me and I fell down over them." There was truth in these flings. I cut twenty thousand words out of the Philadelphia article and then had not written half my facts. I know a man who is making a history of the corrupt construction of the Philadelphia City Hall, in three volumes, and he grieves because he lacks space. You can't put all the known incidents of the corruption of an American city into a book.

This is all very unscientific, but then, I am not a scientist. I am a journalist. I did not gather with indifference all the facts and arrange them patiently for permanent preservation and laboratory analysis. I did not want to preserve, I wanted to destroy the facts. My purpose was no more scientific than the spirit of my investigation and reports; it was, as I said above, to see if the shameful facts, spread out in all their shame, would not burn through our civic shamelessness and set fire to American pride. That was the journalism of it. I wanted to move and to convince. That is why I was not interested in all the facts, sought none that was new, and rejected half those that were old. I often was asked to expose something suspected. I couldn't; and why should I? Exposure of the unknown was not my purpose. The people: what they will put up with, how they are fooled, how cheaply they are bought, how dearly sold, how easily intimidated, and how led, for good or for evil — that was the inquiry, and so the significant facts were those only which everybody in each city knew, and of these, only those which everybody in every other town would recognize, from their common knowledge of such things, to be probable. But these, understated, were charged always to the guilty persons when individuals were to blame, and finally brought home to the people themselves, who, having the power, have also the responsibility, they and those they respect, and those that guide them.

This was against all the warnings and rules of demagogy. What was the result? After Joseph W. Folk had explored and exposed, with convictions, the boodling of St. Louis, the rings carried an election. "Tweed Days in St. Louis" is said to have formed some public sentiment against the boodlers, but the local newspapers had more to do with that than *McClure's Magazine*. After the Minneapolis grand jury had exposed and the courts had tried and the common juries had convicted the grafters there, an election showed that public opinion was formed. But that one election was regarded as final. When I went there the men who had led the reform movement were "all through." After they had read the "Shame of Minneapolis," however, they went back to work, and they have perfected a plan to keep the citizens informed and to continue the fight for good government. They saw, these unambitious, busy citizens, that it was "up to

them," and they resumed the unwelcome duties of their citizenship. Of resentment there was very little. At a meeting of leading citizens there were honest speeches suggesting that something should be said to "clear the name of Minneapolis," but one man rose and said very pleasantly, but firmly, that the article was true; it was pretty hard on them, but it was true and they all knew it. That ended that.

When I returned to St. Louis and rewrote the facts, and, in rewriting, made them just as insulting as the truth would permit, my friends there expressed dismay over the manuscript. The article would hurt Mr. Folk; it would hurt the cause; it would arouse popular wrath.

"That was what I hoped it would do," I said.

"But the indignation would break upon Folk and reform, not on the boodlers," they said.

"Wasn't it obvious," I asked, "that this very title, 'Shamelessness,' was aimed at pride; that it implied a faith that there was self-respect to be touched and shame to be moved?"

That was too subtle. So I answered that if they had no faith in the town, I had, and anyway, if I was wrong and the people should resent, not the crime, but the exposure of it, then they would punish, not Mr. Folk, who had nothing to do with the article, but the magazine and me. Newspaper men warned me that they would not "stand for" the article, but would attack it. I answered that I would let the St. Louisans decide between us. It was true, it was just; the people of St. Louis had shown no shame. Here was a good chance to see whether they had any. I was a fool, they said. "All right," I replied. "All kings had fools in the olden days, and the fools were allowed to tell them the truth. I would play the fool to the American people."

The article, published, was attacked by the newspapers; friends of Mr. Folk repudiated it; Mr. Folk himself spoke up for the people. Leading citizens raised money for a mass meeting to "set the city right before the world." The mayor of the city, a most excellent man, who had helped me, denounced the article. The boodle party platform appealed for votes on the strength of the attacks in "Eastern magazines." The people themselves contradicted me; after the publication, two hundred thousand buttons for "Folk and Reform" were worn on the streets of St. Louis.

But those buttons were for "Folk and Reform." They did go to prove that the article was wrong, that there was pride in St. Louis, but they proved also that that pride had been touched. Up to that time nobody knew exactly how St. Louis felt about it all. There had been one election, another was pending, and the boodlers, caught or to be caught, were in control. The citizens had made no move to dislodge them. Mr. Folk's splendid labors were a spectacle without a chorus, and, though I had met men who told me the people were with Folk, I had met also the grafters, who cursed only Folk and were building all their hopes on the assumption that "after Folk's term" all would be well again. Between these two local views no outsider could choose. How could I read a strange people's hearts? I took the outside view, stated the facts both ways, — the right verdicts of the juries and the confident plans of the boodlers, — and the result was, indeed, a shameless state of affairs for which St. Louis, the people of St. Louis, were to blame.

And they saw it so, both in the city and in the State, and they ceased to be spectators. That article simply got down to the self-respect of this people. And who was hurt? Not St. Louis. From that moment the city has been determined and active, and boodle seems to be doomed. Not Mr. Folk. After that, his nomination for Governor of the State was declared for by the people, who formed Folk clubs all over the State to force him upon his party and theirs, and thus insure the pursuit of the boodlers in St. Louis and in Missouri too. Nor was the magazine hurt, or myself. The next time I went to St. Louis, the very men who had raised money for the mass meeting to denounce the article went out of their way to say to me that I had been right, the article was true, and they asked me to "do it again." And there may be a chance to do it again. Mr. Folk lifted the lid off Missouri for a moment after that, and the State also appeared ripe for the gathering. Moreover, the boodlers of State and city have joined to beat the people and keep them down. The decisive election is not till the fall of 1904, and the boodlers count much on the fickleness of public opinion. But I believe that Missouri and St. Louis together will prove then, once for all, that the people can rule — when they are aroused.

The Pittsburg article had no effect in Pittsburg, nor had that on Philadelphia any results in Philadelphia. Nor was any expected there. Pittsburgh, as I said in the article, knew itself, and may pull out of its disgrace, but Philadelphia is contented and seems hopeless. The accounts of them, however, and indeed, as I have said, all of the series, were written, not for the cities described, but for all our cities; and the most immediate response came from places not mentioned, but where similar evils existed or similar action was needed. Thus Chicago, intent on its troubles, found useless to it the study of its reform, which seems to have been suggestive elsewhere, and Philadelphia, "Corrupt and Contented," was taken home in other cities and seems to have made the most lasting impression everywhere.

But of course the tangible results are few. The real triumph of the year's work was the complete demonstration it has given, in a thousand little ways, that our shamelessness is superficial, that beneath it lies a pride which, being real, may save us yet. And it is real. The grafters who said you may put the blame anywhere but on the people, where it belongs, and that Americans can be moved only by flattery, — they lied. They lied about themselves. They, too, are American citizens; they too, are of the people; and some of them also were reached by shame. The great truth I tried to make plain was that which Mr. Folk insists so constantly upon: that bribery is no ordinary felony, but treason, that the "corruption which breaks out here and there and now and then" is not an occasional offense, but a common practice, and that the effect of it is literally to change the form of our government from one that is representative of the people to an oligarchy, representative of special interests. Some politicians have seen that this is so, and it bothers them. I think I prize more highly than any other of my experiences the half-dozen times when grafting politicians I had "roasted," as they put it, called on me afterwards to say, in the words of one who spoke with a wonderful solemnity:

"You are right. I never thought of it that way, but it's right. I don't know whether you can do anything, but you're right, dead right. And I'm all wrong. We're all, all wrong. I don't see how we can stop it now; I don't see how I can change. I can't, I guess. No, I can't, not

now. But, say, I may be able to help you, and I will if I can. You can have anything I've got."

So you see, they are not such bad fellows, these practical politicians. I wish I could tell more about them: how they have helped me; how candidly and unselfishly they have assisted me to facts and an understanding of the facts, which, as I warned them, as they knew well, were to be used against them. If I could — and I will some day — I should show that one of the surest hopes we have is the politician himself. Ask him for good politics; punish him when he gives bad, and reward him when he gives good; make politics pay. Now, he says, you don't know and you don't care, and that you must be flattered and fooled — and there, I say, he is wrong. I did not flatter anybody; I told the truth as near as I could get it, and instead of resentment there was encouragement. After "The Shame of Minneapolis," and "The Shamelessness of St. Louis," not only did citizens of these cities approve, but citizens of other cities, individuals, groups, and organizations, sent in invitations, hundreds of them, "to come and show us up; we're worse than they are."

We Americans may have failed. We may be mercenary and selfish. Democracy with us may be impossible and corruption inevitable, but these articles, if they have proved nothing else, have demonstrated beyond doubt that we can stand the truth; that there is pride in the character of American citizenship; and that this pride may be a power in the land. So this little volume, a record of shame and yet of self-respect, a disgraceful confession, yet a declaration of honor, is dedicated, in all good faith, to the accused — to all the citizens of all the cities in the United States.

Arthur P. Dudden: THE SHAME OF THE CITIES REVISITED:
PHILADELPHIA

In his paper, "Lincoln Steffens's Philadelphia," Professor Arthur Dudden takes Steffens' analysis of corruption and finds it essentially valid as applied to Philadelphia. Dudden grants that there are defects in Steffens' indictment but basically the muckraker told the magazine-reading public the truth about Philadelphia.

"MY REPORT on 'Philadelphia: Corrupt and Contented,'" Lincoln Steffens wrote in his *Autobiography* (1931), "seemed to give the impression which lasts to this day, that that beautiful old American city was the worst in the land. *Not true, of course.* It was only older than St. Louis and Minneapolis, and I might have shown that and put Philadelphia in its relative position, if I had gone from there to Boston or some other old town in New England; Boston was the next logical step. But my editorial associates on *McClure's* opposed my choice as they did my theory. They were for Chicago next."

So Steffens went off to Chicago in search of "the sensationally wicked story" his associates wanted. To his astonishment, Chicago displayed "an example of reform, a sensible, aristocratic-democratic reform experiment." Learning therefrom that his readers "were interested in reform quite as much as they were in graft," reporter Steffens realized that it "would be good journalism to find and report immediately an experiment in good government to parallel the Chicago experiment in representative government." New York City under Mayor Seth Low was the logical choice. Unfor-

tunately the November election of 1903 returned Tammany Hall to power, and presumably to Tweed-like grafting. Steffens' article on New York City, written on the election's eve, was subtitled "Good Government in Danger" as the result of his fears for the outcome.

The Shame of the Cities (1904), which brought Steffens' sensational articles together in book form, blamed the misgovernment of America's municipalities primarily on their businessmen. Steffens charged: "The typical business man is a bad citizen; he is busy. If he is a 'big business man' and very busy, he does not neglect, he is busy with politics, oh, very busy and very business-like. . . . He is a self-righteous fraud, this big business man. He is the chief source of corruption, and it were a boon if he would neglect politics. But he is not the business man that neglects politics; that worthy is the good citizen, the typical business man. He too is busy, he is the one that has no use and therefore no time for politics. . . . The business man has failed in politics as he has in citizenship."

Here then is the message of Lincoln Steffens. He saw America's cities at the dawn of the twentieth century as shame-

From Arthur Dudden, "Lincoln Steffens's Philadelphia," *Pennsylvania History*, Volume XXXI, October, 1964, Number 4, pp. 449–458. Reprinted by permission of *Pennsylvania History* and of the author.

ful examples of popular misrule. Businessmen were the outstanding culprits, "big" businessmen who distorted democratic means for plutocratic ends, and "typical" businessmen who scorned politics only to fail as citizens. The entire system consisted of vicious circles of special privilege, fostered by civic neglect, and abetted by a popular hypocrisy which deplored politics and lauded business. Perhaps the most enduring portion of his indictment, when reduced to its particulars, was his all-too-happy alliteration for Philadelphia as "corrupt and contented." Philadelphia was "not merely corrupt, but corrupted."

Historians willing to take another look must confront the lack of any important history of Philadelphia for the period of which Steffens wrote. Also they ought to consider the working hypothesis which emerged in Steffens' outlook, while he moved about from city to city. He began to be convinced, he tells in his *Autobiography,* that the age of a city afforded a positive correlation with its hopelessness. Conversely his colleagues on the magazine, he believed, harbored the opposing idea that America's municipal corruption was the worst in the world simply because of this nation's youthfulness. Maturity would eventually bring improvements and social progress, they thought. Instead Steffens was convinced that, with the greater and greater passage of time, the corrupting influences of urban life became cemented into a city's everlasting foundations. "England was our fate, not our hope," he avowed, because of the older country's accumulated handicaps of advanced age. Here he reflected a point-blank disagreement with James Bryce and E. L. Godkin, both of whom anticipated America's urban future optimistically once the current era of crude adolescence reached its end.

Admittedly these are the autobiographical recollections of that Steffens who after 1920 became convinced of the futility of liberal reforms and of the historic truthfulness of the Russian experiment under Lenin and Stalin.

Yet this pessimistic anticipation of worse things due to come serves to explain Steffens' assertion that Philadelphia was not merely corrupt, but corrupted irretrievably into a contented euphoria, a condition which approximated senility for an entire city. It explains also his wish to push on from Philadelphia to Boston, where seniority alone presumably would elevate the Hub City to Steffens' primary rank of corruption. It does not explain, however, his comparatively gentle treatment of New York City, unless he ignored the fact that Father Knickerbocker's metropolis was more ancient than Billy Penn's Philadelphia, an oversight which seems unlikely.

At any rate, we need now to know what were Philadelphia's characteristics and conditions of life in 1900 or thereabout. We must also inquire where "the Philadelphia story" fits into the historic experience of the cities of the United States. From among the myriad items of information obtainable, certain categories stand out as particularly useful for an analysis of Philadelphia's affairs at the beginning of the present century.

First, there is the subject of modern Philadelphia's political dimensions. Until the middle of the past century, the territory of the county of Philadelphia was under the control of approximately thirty municipal corporations of varying areas and populations. Turbulent inter-neighborhood rivalries and clashes between ethnic groups erupted repeatedly, with the volunteer fire companies mixed up conspicuously in these fracases. Then, in 1854, the "Consolidation Act" created

"The City of Philadelphia," largely as it is today, but it continued the county of Philadelphia as one of Pennsylvania's counties, the territory involved possessing a perplexing duality thereafter as the county of Philadelphia and also as the city of Philadelphia. It seems almost needless to point out that conflicts arising between Philadelphia's overlapped jurisdictions, and politically as between the offices of the city's mayor, councilmen, and ward leaders on the one hand, and the county's sheriff, courts, and assessors on the other, have provided a continuing theme for the Quaker City's political life and its corruptions into the present day.

Second, there is the story of Philadelphia's rapid population growth during the second half of the nineteenth century, and the flight into suburban areas which was stimulated by industrial, demographic, and technological pressures or innovations. The census for Philadelphia in round figures reached upward to 675,000 persons in 1870 after expanding nearly 20 per cent during the decade preceding, then increased to 850,000 in 1880, and in 1890 to 1,050,000. By 1900 Philadelphia's population approximated 1,300,000, and then rose to 1,550,000 by 1910 — a tripling of the total of fifty years before. Yet no full notion of the city's enlarging magnitude can be comprehended without an examination of growths taking place simultaneously in adjoining territory. As Ellis Paxson Oberholtzer observed at the close of the new century's first decade: "The lines of settlement have been extended far outside the limits of the county, along the arteries of cheap and rapid passenger transportation. Camden and the trains of New Jersey pour their plenty into Philadelphia each morning and receive it back again at night. On the main line of the Pennsylvania Railroad, north and south and west on all the railway lines, old towns have increased in size and new ones have appeared."

With some qualifications suited to local circumstances, Philadelphia's experience of internal growth and its expansion beyond the legally measured municipal limits was typical of many older cities. Sam B. Warner, Jr. has aptly summarized the reasons for America's suburban trends in his recent study of Boston's growth: "The physical deterioration of old neighborhoods, the crowding of factory, shop, and tenement in the old central city, the unceasing flow of foreigners with ever new languages and habits — these negative pressures tended to drive the middle class from the city. The new technology . . . enabled these families to move out from the old city boundaries into an expanded area of vacant and lightly settled land. In this new land the rural ideal, by its emphasis on the pleasures of private family life, on the security of a small community setting, and on the enjoyment of natural surroundings, encouraged the middle class to build a wholly new residential environment: the modern suburb."

Nor was this novel suburban sprawl solely a residential phenomenon, as the rising, industrial importance of Camden, Norristown, and the Delaware's downriver communities including Chester and Wilmington attested. "It was the metropolitan district, combining the output of urban and suburban factories," Blake McKelvey has demonstrated in his study *The Urbanization of America,* "that best reflected the cumulative advance of the American economy." Philadelphia's growth by 1900, like that of numerous cities, was crowding the older quarters, consuming the open spaces, and exploding beyond the legal boundaries, with a significance that must still be further explored.

Hence the *third* category of relevant information consists of politics, Philadelphia politics, Pennsylvania politics, even national politics. Lincoln Steffens himself led the way. "My theory now," he described his turn from the shamefulness of the cities to the corruptions of state governments, "was that the state was the unit of action for good or evil." In Pittsburgh he had been induced to believe that: "The political business ring which ran the city and linked up with the Matt Quay ring which ran the state belonged to and protected the Pennsylvania Railway." The "trails of evidence" uncovered for him by local individuals "often ran off by way of Harrisburg, the capital city of Pennsylvania, to Philadelphia, the metropolis."

The central feature of Pennsylvania's politics after the Civil War was the Republican Party's domination of the commonwealth. The Republicans won their ascendancy during the war years, and were able for a long time thereafter to exploit that fact. Also Pennsylvania in general endorsed tariff protectionism, and her business community grew attached to the party which elevated this doctrine into a high principle of national wisdom. Bryan's free-silver heresy sharply focused the images of the two major parties held by businessmen and middle-class voters. A clear choice was afforded between the patriotic, prudent, and sane Republicans and the once treasonable and always dangerous Democrats. The Union League, the citadel of stalwart Republicanism, did nothing to dispel these illusions.

Moreover Pennsylvania's Republican Party leadership exploited its opportunities to the hilt. An extraordinary dynasty of bosses held sway. Beginning with the election of Simon Cameron to the United States Senate in 1866, and continuing with his son Donald Cameron, Matthew S. Quay, and until the death of Boies Penrose in 1921, Pennsylvania was ruled by these bosses through the Republican Party. "Able, adroit, masterful, and unscrupulous," Professor Dunaway once described them, "they headed the majority party, which they kept subservient to their domination; controlling federal, state, and local patronage and possessing always a generous campaign fund, their power was supreme. . . . Except for the brief intervals when insurgency raised its head in partial triumph, this powerful political machine proved to be an effective steam roller which regularly flattened out all opposition with thoroughness and dispatch."

The opposition grew enfeebled, particularly in Philadelphia where businessmen joined ranks to maintain tariff protection above all other considerations. In addition their own tendency toward removal to the suburbs outside Philadelphia's political arena, where the city's votes were cast and counted, constituted a self-imposed process of exile, which deprived the city of many of its leading citizens and of that class of men who in earlier times had been responsible for a stewardship over civic affairs. The balance of power in the city tipped into the hands of corruptible masses of impecunious immigrant, Negro, and older-stock voters, who so desperately needed whatever favors the party bosses dispensed that they delivered their sovereign votes as directed. Meanwhile the hapless Democrats became subservient to the majority party for undercover favors and crumbs of patronage.

The *fourth*, and final, category embodies the history of Philadelphia's corruption, a record noticeably similar in many respects to that of several American cities.

In 1889, James Bryce's *The American Commonwealth* described in detail how it had come about that all of the municipal departments obeyed James McManes, who at that time was "the recognized Boss of Philadelphia." McManes and his confederates worked their stranglehold through the municipally-owned gas supply. Their tentacles reached out to control the other municipal offices and officeholders, the police, the city councils, and often the mayors as well. They also obtained control over the principal street tramway company. Thus McManes and his cohorts, as Bryce observed, "became not merely indispensable to the Republican Party in the city, but in fact its chiefs." "Jim" McManes commanded the votes of thousands of municipal and public service employees, and he also enlisted their off-duty energies in unrelenting electioneering to round up additional thousands. Even the officials of the United States Government in the customs-house and post office were coerced into "a dependent alliance" with Philadelphia's political chieftains, whose "support was so valuable to the leaders in Federal politics that it had to be purchased by giving them their way in city affairs."

Against this knavish state of affairs, successive reform movements raged and struggled. The State legislature afforded scant help, as is not surprising. Pennsylvania's legislature was notoriously corrupt, having mortgaged itself early to the railway, coal, petroleum, and manufacturing interests of the state. "The Standard Oil Company has done everything with the legislature of Pennsylvania," Henry Demarest Lloyd avowed, "except refine it." In addition the legislature was responsive to the coercive pressures which were applied by the political machines and their bosses, the state's Republican machine and also Philadelphia's.

Nevertheless reformers scored some

modest gains over the years, or at any rate improvements and achievements of a positive nature did take place. The spectacular centennial celebration of 1876 and the almost forgotten, though very large, centennial celebration of 1887, nurtured and preserved a core of civic pride and performance. So also did the development of Philadelphia's magnificent public parks and parkways, and even the slow graft-ridden erection of City Hall which was capped at long last by Alexander Calder's gigantic statue of William Penn. Meanwhile, reformers continued to toil and spin. Beginning in 1871 with the Citizens' Municipal Reform Association and bearing fruit in 1887 from the efforts of Governor Robert E. Pattison and the Committee of One Hundred, a unique blend of an elite group in the Democratic Party and the generally "wholesome power" of civic minded persons, the so-called "Bullit Charter" took effect for Philadelphia to provide for a strong and, hopefully, independent mayor. The sad truth, however, was that the party machinery provided the mayoralty candidates for a long time thereafter, with little relaxation of bossism's grip on the city. Not until the administration of Mayor Rudolph Blankenburg (1911–1915) did Philadelphia experience forthrightly honest leadership. Even then, the domination of Pennsylvania by its statewide machine was scarcely dented.

Therefore, in major insights, Lincoln Steffens was correct about Philadelphia. The city was a corrupted municipality in 1903. In varying degrees it had been corrupt ever since the Civil War, and perhaps even before then. Both the self-serving activities and the irresponsible negligence of businessmen had contributed to this state of affairs, as Steffens claimed.

If Philadelphia's record was outstandingly bad, the main causes appear to have originated neither with the contentment of its citizens nor with the city's greater age. Philadelphia's troubles, typical enough in themselves, were aggravated by Pennsylvania's unique combination of one-party rule and protectionist politics. Pennsylvania's hierarchy of entrenched Republican Party bosses, United States Senators all of them, dominated the state for three-quarters of a century. Philadelphia's bosses and their compliant voters supported the state's machine, which nourished and sustained them in turn. Against so entrenched an establishment, reformers tilted almost in vain. Their modest achievements came only when they gained a momentary ascendency at the state level, and eventually when the general tone of local politics improved overall. The state, not the city, was the effective unit for good or evil, as Lincoln Steffens himself quickly realized.

Any evaluation of Lincoln Steffens and his story of Philadelphia's municipal corruption would have to affirm that he was indeed right, though not for all, nor for enough of, the right reasons. His reputation for originality and thoroughness seems vastly overrated, when his work is contrasted with what James Bryce and local reformers had been saying all along. He overlooked too many dynamic trends and popular currents in American life. Especially did he underplay the importance of state and national politics for municipal affairs. However, his flair for expressing the mood of popular indignation against the excesses of business and democracy's shortcomings was unequalled. He was unsurpassed in his ability to sum up in a few words for his countrymen what it was they had discovered to be unspeakably odious in their midst. Philadelphia was more restless and turbulent than it was content. But God knows it was corrupt, and Lincoln Steffens shouted this fact unforgettably once and for all to hear — and to be ashamed that this was so!

Samuel P. Hays: THE SHAME OF THE CITIES REVISITED:
THE CASE OF PITTSBURGH

Professor Samuel P. Hays has written extensively of American history in the age of industrialization and city growth. In his paper, "The Shame of the Cities Revisited: The Case of Pittsburgh," *he challenges Lincoln Steffens's view of municipal corruption and the reform movement. According to Hays, Pittsburgh does not conform to the pattern presented by Steffens.*

LINCOLN STEFFENS' classic, *The Shame of the Cities*, has played a major role in establishing our conception of municipal politics in the Progressive Era. The urban political struggle of that time, so the argument goes, pitted public

From Samuel P. Hays, *"The Shame of the Cities* Revisited: The Case of Pittsburgh." Reprinted by permission of the author.

impulses against a corrupt alliance of "machine" politicians and "special interests." This view, for purposes of analysis, can be broken down into three major arguments. First, the *source* of reform lay in the general public rather than in particular groups and represented a broad popular drive rather than limited demands. Second, the reform *target of attack* was the corrupt individual, the political or business leader who because of personal failings made private arrangements at the expense of the public. And third, the *political innovations* brought about by reform consisted of the expansion of popular participation in the governmental process.

Here I will consider this line of reasoning as it pertains to the city of Pittsburgh. On all three counts, I will argue, it is incorrect. Reformers came not from a broad lower or middle class, but from a small elite segment of society. They attacked not a corrupt alliance of political and business leaders, but a decentralized, small community, ward system of government and the political power of the lower and middle classes which that system enhanced. And they sought not to expand, but to limit popular participation in municipal government. This argument rests upon an examination of the personal backgrounds and institutional connections of over 1100 Pittsburgh political leaders of whom two-thirds were reformers, members of the Civic Club and the Voters' League, and one-third their opponents, members of the city's school boards and municipal councils whose power reformers sought to eliminate.

I

Pittsburgh municipal reformers came primarily from the upper class. Of the total of 745, 65 per cent appeared in elite directories which contained the names

of only 2 per cent of the city's families Moreover, a large proportion not in elite directories lived in upper-class areas These reformers comprised not an old but a new elite; few came from earlie industrial and mercantile families. Mos had risen to social position from wealth created after 1870 in the iron, steel, elec trical equipment and other industries and lived in newer rather than olde fashionable areas.

Almost half, 48 per cent, of the reform ers were professionals: doctors, lawyers ministers, directors of libraries and mu seums, engineers, architects, private and public school teachers and college pro fessors. Some of these overlapped with the elite, especially the lawyers, minister and private school teachers, but fo the most part their interest in reform stemmed from the inherent dynamics o their professions rather than their clas connections. Moreover, they came from the more advanced segments of thei organizations. They constituted not olde professionals seeking to preserve the pas against change, but men in the forefron of innovation in professional life, activel seeking to apply expertise more widel to public affairs.

The reformers included a third group 52 per cent were businessmen or thei wives: merchants, bankers, corporatio officials. They included the presidents o fourteen large banks and corporation offi cials of Westinghouse, Pittsburgh Plat Glass, U. S. Steel and its component part such as Carnegie Steel, American Bridg and National Tube, Jones and Laughlin lesser steel companies such as Crucible Pittsburgh, Superior, Lockhart and H. K Porter, the H. J. Heinz Company and th Pittsburgh Coal Company, as well as offi cials of the Pennsylvania Railroad and the Pittsburgh and Lake Erie. Not smal businessmen, these men directed the most powerful banking and industrial organizations of the city. They represented not the old business community, but industries which had developed and grown primarily within the past fifty years and which had come to dominate the city's economic life.

All of these groups, deeply involved in innovation associated with industrialization, were rapidly expanding the geographical scope of their affairs. This, in turn, gave rise to an interest in a new municipal government of similar breadth of action. Members of the new elite, for example, were establishing their separate exclusive social institutions in the East End, previously a relatively uninhabited area. But they could not move with them their economic institutions which remained in the central city. To protect and expand these the elite could not remain satisfied with dominance in its own residential wards but became drawn into an active interest in larger municipal affairs and sought to create a government oriented toward the larger city rather than ward communities.

Professional groups were also broadening the scope of affairs which they sought to study, measure or manipulate. Increasingly they came to look upon their particular professional specialization as representing an aspect of society which they should manipulate to promote change. Schoolteachers pressed for innovations in methods of teaching, an expanded curriculum, more professional training for teachers and greater financial support for the schools. They urged that control of school affairs be shifted from the ward to a city-wide school board with a greater geographical perspective and more accessible to influence from professionals. A similar impulse motivated doctors concerned with public health, engineers with public works con-

struction, architects interested in urban design, leaders of civic institutions who wished to expand libraries and art museums. All of these groups increasingly defined the dimensions of their concerns as city-wide, capable of being dealt with only by a centralized city-wide agency — government — which would have the power and responsibility for positive programs of innovations.

Finally, the new industrial community also began to define its concerns in broader geographical terms. The increasing size and scope of industry, the greater stake in more varied and geographically dispersed facets of the city, the effect of floods of the three rivers on many business concerns, the need to promote traffic flows to and from work for both blue-collar and managerial employees — all these expanded the scope of perspective of the Pittsburgh industrialist from a limited section of the community to the entire city and gave rise to an interest in a municipal decision-making system of similar scope. In the Progressive Era the Pittsburgh Chamber of Commerce expressed these larger economic concerns; it represented those groups which carried out city-wide activities, as contrasted to the more limited interests of small shopkeepers in sub-communities of the city. The Pittsburgh Chamber became a major instrument of municipal reform.

II

All of these groups expressed dissatisfaction with Pittsburgh's government. Yet they opposed not its corruption per se — although there was plenty of that — but its structure, which enabled local and particularistic interests to dominate. City government prior to the municipal reforms of 1910–11 consisted of a confederation of local wards, each one represented on the two bodies of the city council. Each ward, moreover, had its own elementary schools and ward-elected school boards which administered them. These particularistic interests were the focus of a decentralized political life. The occupational composition of the school board and the city council shortly before the successful drive for municipal reform reveals this localized character of government. Of 387 members of these bodies only 24 per cent represented the same managerial, professional, banker and wholesale occupations who had so-called "large interests" and who dominated reform groups; these, for the most part, came from the upper-class wards. The great majority — 67 per cent — were small businessmen, white-collar workers such as clerks, and skilled and unskilled workmen, none of whom were represented in reform groups.

Because of their involvement in the ward's community institutions these men had become local leaders. They spoke for their local areas, the economic interests of their inhabitants, their residential concerns, their educational, recreational and religious interests — i.e., for those aspects of community life which mattered most to their inhabitants. They rolled logs in the city council to provide streets, sewers and other public works for their communities. They looked upon the ward school as a community social center responsive only to limited local concerns for education. They defended the community's cultural practices such as its distinctive languages or national customs, its liberal attitude toward liquor and its saloons and dance halls which served as centers of community life. In short pre-reform officials spoke for their constituencies, inevitably their own wards which had elected them, rather

than for other sections of the city or for groups organized on a city-wide basis.

The most visible opposition to reform attack was, logically, the so-called "machine." For through the "machine" many different ward communities as well as lower and middle income groups joined effectively to influence the central city government whose power might be of use to them. Their own private occupational and social life did not naturally involve these groups in larger city-wide activities in the same way as it did for the elite, and therefore they did not have available privately organized economic and social power on the basis of which they could construct political power. The "machine" filled this organizational gap. Yet it should never be forgotten that the social and economic institutions in the wards themselves provided the "machine's" sustaining support and gave it larger significance. When reformers attacked the machine as the most visible institutional element of that system they attacked the entire ward system of political organization and the political power of lower and middle income groups which lay behind it.

This decentralized system of urban growth and the institutions which arose from it reformers now opposed. Social, professional and economic life had proceeded not only in the local wards on a local scale, but also on a larger scale had become highly integrated and organized. By the early twentieth century those involved in the latter process found the decentralized system of political life limiting to their larger objectives. The movement for reform, therefore, constituted an attempt by upper-class, advanced professional and large business groups to shift formal political power from the previously dominant lower and middle class elements so that their own conceptions of desirable public policy could prevail. These two groups came from entirely different urban worlds, and the political system fashioned by one was no longer acceptable to the other.

Pittsburgh municipal reformers, it should be stressed, looked upon the deficiencies of pre-reform political leaders not in terms of their personal shortcomings, but of the limitation inherent in their occupational, institutional and class positions. In 1911 the Voters' League wrote in its pamphlet analyzing the qualifications of candidates that "a man's occupation ought to give a strong indication of his qualifications for membership on a school board." Certain occupations inherently disqualified a man from serving. "Employment as ordinary laborer and in the lower class of mill work would naturally lead to the conclusion that such men did not have sufficient education or business training to act as school directors. . . . Objection might also be made to small storekeepers, clerks, workmen at many trades, who by lack of educational advantages and business training, could not, no matter how honest, be expected to administer properly the affairs of an educational system, requiring special knowledge, and where millions are spent each year." The League deplored the small number of "men prominent throughout the city in business life . . . in professional occupations . . . holding positions as managers, secretaries, auditors, superintendents and foremen."

III

Reformers, therefore, wished not simply to replace bad men with good, but to change the occupational and class origins of decision makers. Toward this end they proposed innovations in the formal mechanisms of government not to distribute political power through more popular participation in public affairs, but to concentrate it by sharply centralizing the processes of decision-making. Specifically, they hoped to centralize the system of representation by electing city councils and school boards not from wards but from the city at large. Such governing bodies, they argued, would give less attention to local and particularistic matters and more to affairs of city-wide scope. By 1911 Pittsburgh reformers had secured this change for both the city council and the school board. In practice, however, it produced a change not only in the geographical scope of representation, but also in the groups represented. For through city-wide representation those elements privately organized on a city-wide basis, those with large geographical concerns, exercised far more influence in the election of representatives than before and greatly reduced the power of their opponents.

A growing imbalance between population and representation sharpened the desire of reformers to change from ward to city-wide elections. Despite major recent shifts in population within the city neither ward district lines nor the apportionment of city council and school board seats had changed. Consequently, older areas of the city, with wards both small in geographical size and a declining population, enjoyed overrepresentation and newer areas — most notably the East End to which the upper class had moved around the turn of the century — of large size and growing population, became increasingly underrepresented. This sharpened the reformers' conviction that changes in the structure of government would be essential before they could exercise a significant influence on public policy.

The Pittsburgh Chamber of Commerce took the initiative in formulating a plan for the new municipal government. In April 1910 a "New Charter Committee" drew up a "Pittsburgh Plan" of government — a nine-man city council elected at large — and presented it to the state legislature at the next session in 1911. Over 250 men from Pittsburgh appeared at the state capital to support the plan and eleven spoke in its behalf. The few among those whose names are known were representative reformers; eight of the eleven who spoke for the plan were in the Social Register. In order to institute the new system immediately rather than wait for the general election, the governor appointed the new City Council; these nine men also represented the same social, professional and economic groups as did the reformers. For the fall election of 1911 all of the city's political parties renominated all nine appointees who therefore won without opposition. The new city charter, it is significant to note, was not submitted for electoral approval; moreover, by providing for appointment rather than election of the new city council members, reformers secured initial control of the new city government.

The drive for a new school board revealed the same impulse to divorce decision-making from popular influence. A growing pressure from professional teacher organizations, a state educational commission, the Pittsburgh Chamber of Commerce and innovations in other cities produced a demand for a central school board completely independent of the wards, and such a system the Pennsylvania legislature approved in May 1911. The law provided that the new Board of Education be not elected but appointed by the judges of the court of common pleas. Vacancies were to be filled in the same manner. From this time on decisions about educational matters in the city of Pittsburgh remained free from popular electoral control. In the new Pittsburgh Board of Education reformers had succeeded entirely in divorcing a major aspect of government from the ward and class influences which they so strongly opposed.

The composition of the new city council and the school board revealed the degree to which the shift from ward to city-wide representation produced a change in group representation. Members of the upper class, the advanced professionals and the large business groups dominated both. Of the fifteen members of the Pittsburgh Board of Education appointed in 1911 and the nine members of the new city council, none were small businessmen or white-collar workers. Each body contained only one person who could remotely be classified as a blue-collar worker; each of these two filled a position specifically but unofficially designated as reserved for a "representative of labor" and each was an official of the Amalgamated Association of Iron, Steel and Tin Workers. Six of the nine members of the new city council, all prominent businessmen, were listed in elite directories. Two others were doctors closely associated with the upper class in both professional and social life. The fifteen members of the Board of Education included ten businessmen with city-wide interests, one doctor associated with the upper class and three women previously active in upper-class public welfare.

While reformers were divorcing decision-making from popular influence they spoke of their activities in the rhetoric of an extension of popular government. Meetings drawn almost exclusively from the few groups which pushed reform,

and especially from the upper socioeco-
nomic classes, they described as "mass
meetings." The Episcopal Bishop of
Pittsburgh in advocating the new city
council plan before the state legislature
described it as "part of a world-wide
trend toward popular government." Ex-
Mayor George Guthrie maintained at the
same meeting that the proposal "met
with the approval and endorsement of
all people, workingmen, financiers, manufacturers, representatives of Civic Asso-
ciations and the religious life of the community." There is no point in arguing
whether or not such rhetoric was deliberate deception or genuinely believed.
The point is that the evidence of rhetoric
provides no safe guide to the understanding of practice. If we observe what
people did rather than what they said it
becomes clear that Pittsburgh municipal
reformers wished to construct a political
system which would insulate decision-
making further from popular influence.

Steffens, reformers themselves and
later historians misread municipal reform
because they concentrated primarily
upon dramatic episodes and ideological
evidence. In so doing they slighted the
far more important problem of political
structure, of the persistent relationships
of influence and power which grow out
of the community's social, ideological,
economic and cultural activities and the
changes in those relationships. This study
of Pittsburgh municipal reform, I believe, indicates the value of such an approach. For while Steffens and reformers tended to analyze society in terms of
the distribution of morality, selfishness,

rationality or good will, the evidence
here presented indicates that political
life is far more concerned with the distribution of political power which arises
from the patterns of dominance and sub-
ordinance in social, ideological and
economic affairs.

Such an approach, so far as Pittsburgh
is concerned, questions the validity of
both the traditional "people versus the
interests" theory and the more recent
"status" views of reform. For in Pittsburgh at least the impulse for municipal
reform came not from the general public, the "middle class" or an older group
of leaders, but from the new elite, from
professional groups and from large business organizations all deeply involved in
innovation arising from the impulses of
industrialism, science and technology.
They attacked not corruption as such but
an older decentralized ward system of
political organization and the political
power of lower and middle class groups
which this system enhanced. Their most
significant reform was not the greater involvement of the public in political life,
but the shift from a ward to a city-wide
structure of formal government which
shifted political power toward the upper
and professional classes. Municipal reform in Pittsburgh, in short, involved
not a broader distribution of political
power but its concentration, not confidence in the political wisdom of the
"people" but a fear of it and an attempt
to supplant it with a more centralized
formal decision-making process more
responsive to concentrated informal
political power.

In this essay, "The Muckrakers: In Flower and Failure," Louis Filler stresses the need to renew acquaintance with the muckrakers. Muckraking, says Professor Filler, if not fully successful in solving the problems of American society, was a significant affirmation of democracy. The muckrakers did not merely theorize about social issues; they were concerned with practical problem-solving.

ONLY intellectual monopolists will rejoice in the circumstances which have attended muckraking since the First World War and see it as a "field" for solitary tilling and exploitation. If history is a responsibility as well as a trade and is relevant to our society and its operations, then the citizen who happens to be an historian will wish to consider what muckraking has contributed or failed to contribute to our affairs.

It is difficult to say where he might best look. *Contemporary American History, 1877–1913,* by Charles A. Beard (1914), was an interesting survey and was written for the "large numbers of students" whom its author was constantly meeting, who had "no knowledge of the most elementary facts of American history since the Civil War" (page v). But it found no occasion to mention muckraking, even in connection with the passage of the Pure Food Law. Paul Leland Haworth's *America in Ferment* (1915) was more vibrant with a sense of society in motion and of several of its less orthodox leaders; however, it, too, showed no awareness of muckraking, or its dramatic disappearance.

Harold E. Stearns spoke for the new youth, in his *Liberalism in America: Its Origin, Its Temporary Collapse, Its Future* (1919), and eloquently of the descent of liberalism into pragmatic opportunism. But Stearns and his set had cut loose from the grass roots and lacked the simplest knowledge of the actual workings of reform. Their attitude was more than a matter of knowledge; it was a matter of will. They were uninterested in reform. Mark Sullivan, himself one of the old-style liberals, wrote deprecatingly of muckraking in Volumes II and III of his *Our Times* (1927, 1930), attempting, confusedly, to distinguish "sensationalism" from the reporting of "facts," in terms which only a partisan segment of his old co-workers would have accepted.

The Era of the Muckrakers, by C. C. Regier (1932), a doctoral thesis, was braver in title than in treatment. With small grasp and uncertain information, it held muckraking to have been no more than a "fad" — a thing of a season, rather than of an era. John Chamberlain's *Farewell to Reform* (1932) walked progressively away from muckraking; by its last page, it had fully established the "failure of reform," at no more expense than of logic, understanding, facts, and consistency. Silence became the rule thereafter. There were sound and relevant pages in Harold U. Faulkner's *The Quest*

Reprinted with permission, from *Essays in American Historiography,* edited by Donald Sheehan and Harold C. Syrett, pp. 251–268. Copyright © 1960 Columbia University Press.

for Social Justice, 1898–1914 (1931). But even such pages and paragraphs failed to take into account the fact that the subject was heavy with controversy and that no reference to muckraking could be truly sound which did not come to grips with the pertinent pros and cons. . . .

No, the muckrakers are not well remembered. Clichés of accomplishment are, to be sure, still identified with several of their names. Tarbell, Steffens, and Baker, of *McClure's* and the *American,* and a few others in desultory formation, are still cited as notable in an age of exposé, still credited with generous and desirable civic traits. But others are as regularly condemned for intemperateness or shallowness or sensationalism. This would be true of Thomas W. Lawson and David Graham Phillips and Upton Sinclair. A typical and widely used work distinguishes the muckrakers from the progressive movement which it is said to have helped publicize, and even from the "literature of revolt," "a fictional literature dedicated to advancing the cause of democracy." It credits *McClure's* writers with accuracy and readability, but concludes:

It was inevitable, however, that the muckraking technique should be adopted by publishers and writers of dubious integrity and exploited merely for financial gain. As muckraking turned [*sic*] into yellow journalism around 1906, public interest was at first tremendously stimulated. But soon readers tired of the excitement; and by 1908 the entire muckraking movement was discredited.

This study finds a line of distinction between muckrakers and progressives such as the naked eye cannot perceive, though there were muckrakers who preferred Wilson or Debs to Theodore Roosevelt, in 1912. It distinguishes between muckrakers and the "social justice movement," though there were muckrakers active in every one of its folds. Brand Whitlock, for example, was crusader, mayor, and, not incidentally, novelist, and anything but alone in his many-sidedness. The juxtaposition of muckraking and yellow journalism is patently inadequate, and the date of 1908 patently inaccurate. In 1908, the Ballinger affair had not yet taken place. *Hampton's, Everybody's, Collier's, Success,* the *American,* and a dozen other muckraking magazines were still being distributed to mass audiences. But the purpose of these observations is not to argue a point; it is merely to indicate that the muckrakers have not been well remembered.

The greater number of them have been thoroughly forgotten, the few others who are generally cited serving no particular end. They are mere names — Charles Edward Russell, Norman Hapgood, Samuel Hopkins Adams — or mere titles — *The Story of Life Insurance, The Women Who Toil, People of the Abyss, The Color Line.* They fill out the paragraphs in textbooks, or add *décor* to analyses of twentieth-century trends. C. P. Connolly, Josiah Flynt, Herbert N. Casson, Frederic U. Adams, John K. Turner, Benjamin B. Hampton are several of many personages who were significant to, or central in, muckraking operations, and whose names never appear in commentary respecting the era.

But this is not the bottom fact of forgetfulness. The muckrakers' works have not survived their heyday. It is not only that they have not been reprinted; they are unread. This is as true of Lincoln Steffens as of Charles Edward Russell. Many of the muckrakers thought of themselves as literary figures as well as students of society and commentators. They have received regard in neither area. (Ray Stannard Baker is curious in this respect in that his David Grayson books continue to sell to the type of reader who is not influenced by official literary criticism.) Finley Peter Dunne would seem to be an exception to the generalization, in that he is frequently quoted, and in a variety of sources. However, a recent, parochial stir of interest in his work, sponsored by the *New Republic*, only revealed that publication's glaring lack of contact with the reality of Dunne and also the enthusiastic incapacity of its readers.

The loss of contact with the detail of muckraking has affected individual and historical perspective. Thus, Edwin Markham was the poet of reform and also the prophet of the child-labor crusade. The numerous references to his most famous poem have only underscored how completely buried are his achievements as both poet and reformer, to say nothing of his long and significant personal odyssey. How does one assess his work? Is it diminished by comparison with that of the socialists of his time? of the politicos? Does it lose stature when placed beside the writings of the revolutionary youth of the 1910s? Or beside permutations of similar elements in the 1920s or after? The fact is, of course, that these nonmuckraking elements have not themselves escaped the unsympathetic judgment of time. A few reform and radical reputations remain, from the ruins of our past decades: La Follette, Eugene V. Debs, Big Bill Haywood, John Reed, and Randolph Bourne are credited with integrity and accomplishment. But whether any of them are better read than Markham, or *McClure's*, may be questioned.

The reputations of the muckrakers need to be recaptured and described; but even more, they need to be explained. For if it should appear that they represented something real in the American people — something permanent and unavoidable — and reflected it in accurate and connotative terms, it might be that they have been too hastily prejudged and insight into our very own times lost.

Although muckraking suddenly confronted a startled and receptive public, many of its elements were rooted in American attitudes and experiences, extending back to John Peter Zenger's time or beyond. Like earlier reformers, the muckrakers were to blend utopian and sentimental aspirations with hard and immediate concerns. They were to carry over into their crusade remnants of every manner of earlier movement of dissent and so establish a firm continuity with past experience. Cooperatives, Negro rights, socialism, humanitarianism, the nationalization schemes of the Bellamyites, the single tax — these causes and many others were to figure in the work of the muckrakers. Nevertheless, their work contained novelties which stirred their readers and put them into motion.

The muckrakers were not untried or accidentally assembled. A significant percentage of them were mature people, who had accumulated experience on newspapers or with magazines. An equally significant number were from the farm and the west: although muckrakers worked in the cities, muckraking did *not* derive primarily from urban conditions. It was a sophisticated continuation of the old, nineteenth-century revolt which had culminated in Populism. With progressivism, its other self, it used "the same ideas travelling in the same direction, with new leaders, new vitality, and new weapons, against the old forces of privilege and corruption." This statement requires qualification. True, the muckrakers came to New York trailing romantic memories of Republican fathers and families which had been self-reliant, patriotic, and religious. (Upton Sinclair was the scion of a broken Southern family; and, indeed, the South's relationship to muckraking and progressivism has long wanted individual and intensive treatment.) They left regions which were not reconciled to Bryan's defeat. But their vision was broader than that of their Populist predecessors. Writers like Hamlin Garland who could not progress beyond its horizons would be thrust aside by the muckrakers. They had grown up in an untidy and even desperate land: an America of new political entities, of new industry, immigrations, and cities. They had little time for nostalgic recollections of an allegedly golden age of peace and plenty. The major muckrakers could not afford the naive anti-Semitism of the Populists; on the contrary, their experience made them enthusiastic partisans of their newer compatriots. Their America needed many things, but above all, it needed communication. The frontier had been closed with unprecedented rapidity, and the barest minimum of telegraph wires and roads had not yet been completed. The multiplying factories and company towns increasingly employed hands rather than people. The cities burgeoned with neighborhoods which literally could not speak English.

The need for communication — of problems, aims, and simple circumstances — was central to the needs of post-Civil War America. It was not satisfied in the established newspapers and magazines. These, curiously enough, also upheld the values of the Populists, favoring free enterprise and opportunity; unlike the Populists, they refused to recognize factors which had narrowed both beyond endurance. John Hay, once of Indiana and author of *Pike County Ballads,* was of the New York *Tribune* before he ascended to glory, and also the bitter anti-

labor author of *The Bread-Winners.* Charles A. Dana, late secretary of Brook Farm, was now the savagely cynical editor of the New York *Sun,* itself once of the pre-war "penny press" and responsive to its readers' interests. Thomas Nast, who exposed the Tweed Ring, also pelted Horace Greeley ruthlessly with editorial mud, in the interests of Grant's second candidacy. E. L. Godkin, of the *Nation,* was a lucid and determined liberal, whose liberalism, however, tolerated neither radicals nor Grangers.

The future muckrakers, following obscure democratic traces, fell in with the new popular newspapers and magazines, where they could best observe the disorder of post-Civil war American life, and report it without compunction, as news. The newspapers of the 1890s, and even before, are the best sources for pre-muckraking material, and are yet to be fully and intelligibly examined.

The journalism of the future muckrakers especially helps to explain the novel talents which were to give them so much influence over their readers. Steffens on the New York *Post,* that newspaperman's newspaper, experimented freely with ideas and features. He sought writers, not journalists. He encouraged statements of reality rather than conventional formulations. In effect, he looked outward to his reader rather than attempting to foist a preconceived view of affairs upon him. Charles Edward Russell's staff on the New York *World* avoided neither horror nor confusion, and it treated rich and poor as warranting equal attention. *World* writers learned what subjects, details, and choice of words arrested the general reader; as David Graham Phillips put it, in an ill-used novel:

[Howard] saw that his success had been to a great extent a happy accident; that to repeat it, to improve upon it he must study life, study the art of expression. . . . He must work at style, enlarge his vocabulary, learn the use of words, the effect of varying combinations of words both as to sound and as to meaning. "I must learn to write for the people," he thought, "and that means to write the most difficult of all styles."

But as important as newspaper experience were the points of view which the nascent crusaders — working in a hectic milieu of free enterprise and experiment — developed in the course of their work. Unconsciously, they were profiting from a democratic revolution in journalism. For as the new popular press mushroomed in response to mass demand, so new magazines, for the first time in American history seeking popularity in the broad sense, began to find solid footing and to develop programs for common consumption. It needs to be kept in mind that the purpose of *Munsey's, McClure's, Collier's* — those individualistic concerns — was *not* to produce low-grade reading for the lower classes; it was to produce quality magazines at cheaper prices and for a wider audience than the established magazines recognized. And who could produce articles from which the general reader could derive information and ideas having something to do with him and his actual affairs and thus justifying his serious expenditure of perhaps twenty or more cents? Not the Civil War generals who filled *Century* with their memoirs, not the government bureaucrats, the cultural dilettantes, travelers, clubmen, and dreamers whose stories and articles filled *The Forum, Poet-Lore, Scribner's,* and many another publication. The newspapermen who had tramped the streets, reported catastrophes, interviews, elections skullduggery, stock-market developments, building projects, and other happenings in the workaday world, who

had sought human interest stories in obscure corners of the city, were prepared to formulate pieces which were up-to-date, and concerned with living American themes and operations. The new magazines were *not* reform magazines; they were money-making ventures. They were purchased because they gave due regard to the human vocabulary of contemporary affairs. In succeeding, the magazine entrepreneurs forged a weapon of communication, a vehicle for whatever purposes their public might prefer.

From what point of view did the popular reporter write? The Populist would hardly have recognized it. It seemed, essentially, a disenchanted viewpoint. Too much had happened in the Populist's lifetime to leave his successor many illusions. The Darwinian hypothesis compromised much that he had learned at home. His own family troubles — with weather, railroads, monopolistic concerns — infringed upon his optimism. Newspaper work revealed too much that was seamy and uncontrollable. A comparison between Theodore Dreiser and David Graham Phillips is revealing and merits full examination, on its own merits, as well as to neutralize the effects of remarkably misdirected commentary available in the field. That both men came from Indiana is among the minor facts requiring mention. Dreiser was born into a family whose values had been badly frayed by economic and social circumstances and whose relationships had deteriorated. Phillips was the son of a small-town banker, surrounded with loving family and security. Both Dreiser and Phillips entered journalism. Dreiser drifted into it, in the sad, dissatisfied way which would be his trademark. Phillips, out of Princeton, plunged into it, determined to learn the facts of American life. Both young men were in secure, pessimistic, appalled by the indifference and cruelty which their journalistic experiences repeatedly revealed and which Herbert Spencer's philosophy underscored. Early in the 1890s, Phillips managed to write a number of articles and sketches for *Harper's Weekly*. In view of the robust optimism, the indomitable will toward happiness and success which his later fiction and muckraking displayed, his 1890s efforts are strikingly depressed and languid in tone. Phillips was a Bryan Democrat in 1896, but the fiction to which he subscribed was influenced by Zola and naturalistic determinism. Dreiser, oddly enough, had not read Zola, when he began to evolve his somber tales. But he persisted in writing them in the face of the burst of energy and anticipation which muckraking released and for which he had no enthusiasm.

Phillips, on his side, threw over his pessimism and abandoned determinism, to preach with renewed faith the doctrine that the individual counted, that he could make his presence felt, and that society could progress:

The "great battle" was on — the battle he had in his younger days looked forward to and longed for — the battle against Privilege and for a "restoration of government by the people." The candidates were nominated, the platforms put forward and the issue squarely joined.

One needs to recall — as undiscriminating critics have not — that this is from Phillips's first book, published before muckraking went into effect, written hastily while its author carried his daily burden of newspaper and editorial work, to say nothing of his personal conflicts. It is a raw production, valuable for many purposes, but at the other extreme from Phillips's finished work. The present passage says something about the frame of mind which the public now assumed, in the satisfaction it took in muckraking. Was it an unrealistic perspective, conducive to the production of shallow writings? The present author has elsewhere added up some of the notable works written during the reform period, in social criticism, description of contemporary processes, human and individual documentation, fiction, verse, and other fields. It seems more important, here, to consider the effectiveness of muckraking which might, or might not, entitle it to attention, and also to ask what qualities defined or limited it, in its own time or after.

The work which the muckrakers did can only be appreciated when seen beside the fact that there were earnest, principled, determined, and powerful forces which freely opposed democracy, in the pre-First World War period. The articles, books, and other publications frankly and aggressively opposing democratic processes are too numerous, too variegated to indicate. A major point of concern was the immigrant, who appeared to them slave-minded, unable to understand Anglo-Saxon freedom, prone to radicalism, unionism, and general disorder. An added impediment to the maintenance of democratic forms and considerations was the atomization of American society. True, the key elements of monopoly and law operated freely and in harmony in defense of their interest, using, among other ingredients of social control, strikebreakers, the black list, and the antistrike injunction. But more needful social elements were not united, and were often opposed, on the meaning of civil liberties, the relation of law to economic plight, and the rights of minority groups. It is an old paradox that "everybody" opposed trusts and that they nevertheless continued to grow; they continued to grow during the reform era.

Was this a failure of reform? Obviously, the reformers were not agreed on what constituted proper curbs on large business consolidations. The purpose of their writings, however, was not so much catharsis as it was enlightenment: they were providing their public with information — in all its connotative complexity — necessary to determining its wants. The public's decisions were often disappointing. In Upton Sinclair's famous phrase, *The Jungle* had aimed for the public heart and hit it in the stomach. But the public's horrified response to the reality of unclean food is an impressive example of the relationship, in the era of reform, between ideas and action, between writers and the general public. That public did more than feel a guilty involvement in the ugly and antisocial operations which disfigured city and state political organizations, permitting organized crime, thievery by corporations, fraud by insurance combines, inhumanity by real estate interests, and a long series of exploitative devices by employers large and small. The public demanded and received action in the ousting of numerous bosses and political machines, in the enactment of a quite endless number of laws and ordinances, from the famous Pure Food Law of 1906 to laws providing for safety measures and devices in public and private places.

All this did not destroy the corporations. It did not even regulate them. But it surrounded them with a network of laws which permanently established their responsibility to the public in every field, and were an earnest promise of further intervention whenever occasion might require. In rousing common citizens to their own interests and duties, the muckraker reaffirmed the reality of democracy, despite giant business and the mazes of modern social organization; and by giving individuals a stake in affairs which did not concern them directly, he gave them a sense of national responsibility which unified and dignified them, at the expense of the blatant "elitists" who presumed to direct their thinking and activities for them.

It has sometimes been observed that the muckraker seemed to put as high a premium upon the process of exposure as upon the subject being exposed; and it has been concluded that he inadequately appreciated the need to deal competently with particular social problems. Aside from the high competence of muckrakers and reformers in their several fields of inquiry, this criticism misses the mechanism of muckraking, which assumed that nothing could be done of value, permanent or otherwise, which did not start with a regard for freedom of inquiry, freedom of communication, and an impartial control of all elements of society. It is often assumed that muckraking was easy sport. Forgotten is the fact that the leading muckrakers were always in danger of violence, vilification, deliberate plots for character assassination; we will shortly note the classic case of successful libel: a deed of darkness perpetrated in open daylight. This fact assured the highest responsibility of action on the part of the muckrakers. At the very least, they were liable to ruinous law suits; it is a sensational aspect of the era that they were so rarely required to justify themselves in court.

Thus, it was not alone giant thefts, grossly unsanitary methods of manufacture, and corrupt administration of public responsibilities which characterized muckraking, though these were sufficiently noteworthy. It was *the process of social control* which the muckrakers instituted which was a major threat to private interests, a major democratic landmark. This helps explain why later journalistic sensations of the postmuckraking era could seem to be different from those of the tabloid stripe, could look like the original article, and yet lack its original impact and significance. *Collier's* in the 1920s ran numerous series in what seemed to its editors the old tradition, "exposing," for example, the evils of venereal disease. Norman Hapgood, once again an editor in the 1920s, took satisfaction in his exposé of the Ku Klux Klan in *Hearst's International Magazine*. And so many other editors and publications, old and new. But even the still-active editors felt that something had changed since the old days. Their magazines no longer served strategic purposes. They no longer appealed to a cohesive audience, in control of national issues, and jealous of civil liberties. It suffices to recall the extirpation of minority opinion during the First World War, the numerous indignities, and worse, inflicted upon minority groups, and the long, daylight ordeal of Sacco and Vanzetti to realize that muckraking had lost some basic strength and influence. . . .

What had the muckrakers not taken into account? We might, at least, attempt not to let their confusions blind us. The domestic achievements of the first Wilson administration are often noticed. It is less often noticed that the period during which Taft was President had also been notable for a long list of legislative accomplishments. The knowing reader understands immediately that many of these achievements had no particular connection with Taft or his official party. It should be evident that legislative triumphs have no necessary connection with attendant administrations. To that extent the muckrakers were correct to concen-

trate upon men and issues rather than upon theories of bureaucracy. But Herbert Croly was also right, in his famous storehouse of revaluations, when he wrote in scorn of reformers to whom "reform means at bottom no more than moral and political purification." This admirer of Mark Hanna was interested in what he conceived to be a larger program, such as Theodore Roosevelt would, presumably, be able to furnish: a program for the elite, of government intervention wherever required, and, for the less consequential classes, popular unity built around a national ideal.

It is little short of amazing how little thought the muckrakers gave to administrative questions on the national level. They appear to have thought it poor form to examine the personnel with whom the President pleased to surround himself. The People's Lobby which they instituted in 1906 was instrumental in the notable fight against Speaker Cannon of the House of Representatives, but it operated entirely from the outside of government. The muckrakers do not appear to have expected their President to surround himself with Progressives. They accepted Taft as his successor with extraordinary good grace. Their most glaring lack was in the field of foreign affairs. Not that, as a group, they were aggressive nationalists, let alone imperialists. Such muckrakers as Charles Edward Russell were international-minded and antiimperialist in sentiment. But, as a group, they gave too little attention to foreign affairs at all and permitted Roosevelt and Taft to act as they pleased in these matters, and with associates who were bureaucrats and elitists, and even social butterflies, almost to the last man.

In such of their attitudes, the muckrakers, of course, reflected the indifference of the average man to intricate gov-

ernmental affairs. That individual had
developed a high sensitivity to his own
woes and dangers. He had relatively
little attention to spare for foreigners or
for the mechanisms which at home controlled his existence. By 1910, he was
satisfied that the awkward old systems of
boss rule had been overthrown, and that
the old, heavy-handed operations of
trusts were things of the past. Journalists
and reformers appeared to be competing
for his attention; he needed no more
than to choose between them.

No analysis of the precipitous decline
of muckraking would be complete which
did not take in the psychological aspect
of the public's role. But nothing can be
shallower than to believe that the public
"tired" of muckraking. On the contrary,
it assumed that popular magazines, as
well as other vehicles of communication,
were continuing to deal with essentials
in public affairs. It assumed that the
victories of free speech and inquiry were
established. It failed to become concerned when some of the more aggressive magazines issued warning signals
that they were under attack, or to give
more than passing attention to the
phenomenon of magazines closing down
despite subscription lists in the hundreds
of thousands. It remained for John Reed,
a proud young man with no regard for
grass-roots politics or values, and with
his coterie's malicious contempt for
muckraking, to observe sardonically:

> A silly tale I've heard
> That round the town is flying
> That every monthly organ
> Is owned by J. P. Morgan.
> Now isn't that absurd?
> Somebody must be lying.

Symbolic of this critical period was the
overthrowing of La Follette as leader of
the Progressive movement, by methods

which have not yet been adequately
examined. Suffice it here that on the
occasion of his well-known speech, significantly to the Periodical Publishers
Association, on February 2, 1912, La
Follette was maligned from coast to
coast. It was also held that he had
suffered a nervous breakdown and thus
become unavailable for the Presidential
nomination. It is inconceivable that such
an attack could have been maintained
successfully two short years before. The
demand for clarification would have
been such as to drive La Follette's tra-
ducers under cover. In this instance, no
such demand arose. Theodore Roosevelt,
with his supporters led by millionaires
Frank A. Munsey and George W. Perkins, took over the Progressive party and
put it on what seemed to them a more
practical basis. It was now an organization of the political elite.

As the popular magazines settled down
into soft entertainment agencies, uncriti-
cal of society's leaders, undemanding of
their readers, new organs were founded
which did not seek mass circulation and
which concentrated upon programs
rather than popular sentiment. The
Masses did not speak, of course, to the
masses, but to a relatively tiny, if select,
audience. Croly's New Republic was dependent upon private funds. Nevertheless, such publications boasted of intellectual status and influence and did not
mourn the passing of the muckrakers.

The first Woodrow Wilson administration seemed to justify their choice of
exclusiveness, rather than grass-roots
content. It moved smoothly and intelligently. If anything, Wilson was more
aggressive than Roosevelt had been in
fulfilling his tariff, currency, agricultural,
and other promises. Even so, the legislative program of what one might call
the Democratic and Republican Progres-

sive alliance, from 1913 to 1916, was something less world-shaking, in retrospect, than what was unleashed in Europe during that same period. A Clayton Anti-Trust Act which did not shackle trusts, a free trade tariff which, thanks to the European war, among other factors, did not initiate free trade, a Federal Reserve System which proved its metal in 1929, and a Federal Trade Commission which firmly protected businesses which could stand on their own feet — these were harbingers of expanded government responsibilities but hardly justified the eloquence of the 1912 campaign.

The truth is that Progressivism had become an efficiency movement, somewhat comparable, on the side of politics, to the Taylorization movement in industry which was sweeping out old technological and organizational modes from business plants, without necessarily raising concomitant social and economic relations to a more democratic and otherwise valid level.

The harshest thing, then, that one can say of those who succeeded the muckrakers — those who followed Croly's shining lights of the *New Republic* — was not that they were manipulators who planned to dominate affairs from raised platforms. The harshest thing that can be said of them is that they were ineffective: they were insects on the great wheel of events, who persuaded themselves that they were turning it. That Croly and his friends should have scorned the muckrakers and popular reformers as naive and with an inadequate program would be amusing, if it were not so tragic in the light of Croly's own impotence during the First World War and the fight for the League of Nations. All students of the time are acquainted with Wilson's strange and somber proph-

ecy, when he decided for war, that it would stop thought in this country, promote hysteria, and breed popular evils of antidemocratic action. This was the nation for which both the Creel Committee on Public Information, composed largely of ex-muckrakers, and, on a more seemly intellectual level, the Croly elitists, administered the philosophical side of the war. It is curious that the crusade to save democracy abroad should have had, as a concomitant, so much that was less than democratic back home. The Croly intellectuals were, of course, opposed to lynchings, tar-and-feathering parties, and the gentle game which young girls played of pinning white feathers on young men not wearing uniforms. But Croly and his friends had no means for controlling these popular manifestations of patriotism — a patriotism which they had themselves solicited. And their high-level social thinking had less and less relationship to it. In their worries and dissatisfaction with the great crusade we may find the shadow of what would finally become a characteristic of elements of their following: a plaintive and resentful fear of the numerous people who did not read liberal publications and an untiring search for formulas which would curb their intemperate whims.

In the 1920s, it was possible for Croly liberals to remain visible among the forces of the left and the forces of the right which were building at home and abroad. Croly liberalism, separating right from wrong, good from bad, efficiency from inefficiency, seemed to express a natural aristocracy of leadership. It carried the promise of power. To that extent, it was still possible for it to denigrate the old muckraking technique as naive and irrelevant, since it was alleged to have been bemused by old, outmoded

American ideals and experiences, and to be incapable of coping with the pragmatic realities of post-First World War affairs. In the 1930s, however, it began to appear that liberalism might itself be cashiered as irrelevant and that a new principle of control over public action and opinion might be developed out of the compulsive and immediate needs of the insecure masses. But these needs turned out to be more complex than the calculations of doctrinaire intellectuals of any persuasion could predict. The New Deal was a pragmatic patchwork of contradictory programs. It could hardly be anything else, since it was a mere response to apparent needs, rather than to formulated experiences or philosophies, and could be changed and even discarded at will. There was no public controversy when Dr. Win the War was substituted for Dr. New Deal: no explanation of the points on which they differed.

Public policy, like public need, was not formulated in Washington (to say no more of the liberal publications), but estimated by balancing decisive action by foreign governments against public opinion at home. This, public opinion polls were cleverly learning to assay. They could not explain it. The dream of the elitists of forging policy which the manipulated masses would have to accept had been reduced to a process of trying to read its wants and gain its suffrage by promising to act upon them.

This was obviously no policy at all, and such works as Samuel Lubell's *The Future of American Politics* (1952) were efforts to advance beyond mere guesses and promises: to examine the voter's actual purposes and characteristics and to trace the history of his choices. Although this was a scientific approach, it did not always produce scientific results.

The "usable past" was not so easy to find or use. In addition, it did not answer the question of one's convictions. As Grover Cleveland had asked, "What is the use of being elected or reelected, unless you stand for something?" It was a refreshing question, and not indefinitely avoidable.

The intelligence able and willing to meet the question might wish to survey the past decades with a less peremptory attitude toward the experiences they were able to offer. And, among other experiences, it might wish to come to grips with those of the muckrakers. The key difficulty with the intellectuals of liberal movements of the twentieth century since the days of the muckrakers had been that they had cut themselves off from grass-roots relationships and avoided truly pragmatic alliances and understandings. They had dealt in verbalisms. They had taken on modern problems of industry and social relations, in a context of Marxism, Freudism, and other economic and human disciplines, at the expense of direct contact with the people whom they were presuming to analyze and lead. The intellectuals of the 1910s did not supplement muckraking methods and projects with their own insights; they treated them with contempt. The journalists, commentators, analysts of succeeding decades deepened and developed this easy and catastrophic trait. It was, of course, no mere error of judgment. It reflected an effort to avoid parochialism, an effort to meet the challenge of mass production and international anarchy with living programs of social study and techniques of social control. But in taking the larger social setting into its purview, the up-to-date, up-to-the-minute commentator lost control of his domestic circumstances. His choice was not really between New Deal experimentation on a high governmental level, and Progressive intimacy with traditional American ideals and expectations. Both were necessary to a program with reasonable possibilities for fulfillment. If the flowering of muckraking had been an American triumph, its failure had been an American setback. The problem was not to accept or reject muckraking, but to understand it; and first, to recapture its reality.

Richard Hofstadter: THE PROGRESSIVE IMPULSE

Richard Hofstadter's The Age of Reform (1955) *is a major study of the liberal tradition. Muckraking is viewed as an essential component of the Progressive movement and the sources of "the revolution in journalism" are traced. As seen by Professor Hofstadter, muckraking was shaped by the Protestant tradition with its emphasis upon personal guilt and responsibility.*

MUCKRAKING: THE REVOLUTION IN JOURNALISM

TO AN extraordinary degree the work of the Progressive movement rested upon its journalism. The fundamental critical achievement of American Progressivism was the business of exposure, and journalism was the chief occupational source of its creative writers. It is hardly an exaggeration to say that the Progressive mind was characteristically a journalistic mind, and that its characteristic contribution was that of the socially responsible reporter-reformer. The muckraker was a central figure. Before there could be action, there must be information and exhortation. Grievances had to be given specific objects, and these the muckraker supplied. It was . muckraking that brought the diffuse malaise of the public into focus.

The practice of exposure itself was not an invention of the muckraking era, nor did muckraking succeed because it had a new idea to offer. The pervasiveness of graft, the presence of a continuous corrupt connection between business and government, the link between government and vice — there was nothing new in the awareness of these things. Since the 1870's, exposure had been a recurrent theme in American political life. There had been frequent local newspaper crusades. Henry Adams and his brother Charles Francis had muckraked the Erie ring and the "Gold Conspiracy"; *The New York Times, Harper's Weekly,* and Thomas Nast had gone after Tammany in the seventies. There had been a great deal of exposure in the nineties, when Parkhurst and the Lexow Committee were active in New York, and W. T. Stead's *If Christ Came to Chicago* had caused a sensation in that city. Henry Demarest Lloyd's *Wealth against Commonwealth,* published in 1894, was a brilliant piece of muckraking. Hamlin Garland's Populist novel, *A Spoil of Office*, showed how general was the familiarity with state corruption. Indeed, during the last three decades of the nineteenth century, literally dozens upon dozens of novels were published which have been designated, because of their concentration upon corruption, "premuckraking" novels.

What was new in muckraking in the Progressive era was neither its ideas nor its existence, but its reach — its nationwide character and its capacity to draw nationwide attention, the presence of mass muckraking media with national circulations, and huge resources for the research that went into exposure. The muckraking magazines had circulations running into the hundreds of thousands. They were able to pour funds into the investigations of their reporters — S. S. McClure estimated that the famous articles of Ida Tarbell cost $4,000 each and those of Lincoln Steffens $2,000 — and they were able, as very few of the practitioners of exposure had been able before, not merely to name the malpractices in American business and politics, but to name the malpractitioners and their specific misdeeds, and to proclaim the facts to the entire country. It now became possible for any literate citizen to know what barkeepers, district attorneys, ward heelers, prostitutes, police-court magistrates, reporters, and corporation lawyers had always come to know in the course of their business.

Behind muckraking there was a long history of change in journalism, the story of a transformation in the newspaper and magazine world. The immensely rapid urbanization of the country had greatly enlarged daily newspaper circulation. In 1870 there were 574 daily newspapers in the country; by 1899 there were 1,610; by 1909, 2,600. The circulation of daily newspapers increased over the same span of time from 2,800,-000 to 24,200,000. This expansion had opened up to publishers remarkable promotional opportunities, which brought in their train a number of changes in journalistic practice.

The newspaper owners and editors soon began to assume a new role. Experienced in the traditional function of reporting the news, they found themselves undertaking the more ambitious task of creating a mental world for the uprooted farmers and villagers who were coming to live in the city. The rural migrants found themselves in a new urban world, strange, anonymous, impersonal, cruel, often corrupt and vicious, but also full of variety and fascination. They were accustomed to a life based on primary human contacts — the family, the church, the neighborhood — and they had been torn away from these and thrust into a more impersonal environment, in which they experienced a much larger number of more superficial human relationships. The newspaper became not only the interpreter of this environment but a means of surmounting in some measure its vast human distances, of supplying a sense of intimacy all too rare in the ordinary course of its life. Through newspaper gossip it provided a substitute for village gossip. It began to make increased use of the variety and excitement of the city to capture personal interest and offer its readers indirect human contacts. The rural mind, confronted with the city, often responded with shock, and this too the newspaper did not hesitate to exploit. So one finds during the seventies, eighties, and nineties an increasing disposition on the part of editors to use the human-interest story, the crusade, the interview, and the stunt or promotional device to boom circulation. The large newspaper with a growing circulation became less dependent upon the political party. There were more politically independent or quasi-independent papers, and publishers felt more inclined to challenge the political parties and other institutions. In business terms the benefits to booming circulation of crusades and exposés far outstripped the dangers from possible retaliation. In an age when news was at a premium and when more and more copy was needed to surround the growing columns of advertisement, there was a tendency for publishers and editors to be dissatisfied with reporting the news and to attempt to make it. The papers made news in a double sense; they created reportable events, whether by sending Nelly Bly around the world or by helping to stir up a war with Spain. They also elevated events, hitherto considered beneath reportorial attention, to the level of news occurrences by clever, emotionally colored reporting. They exploited human interest, in short. This was something that had existed almost from the beginning of the popular penny press — one remembers, for instance, the elder James Gordon Bennett's capacity to exploit his own flamboyant personality. But the new exploitation of human interest was different. There was more of it, of course, and it was more skillfully done, but, most symptomatic, there was a change in its character. Where the old human interest had played up the curious concern of the common citizen with the affairs and antics of the rich, the new human interest exploited far more intensely the concern of comfortable people with the affairs of the poor. The slum sketch, the story of the poor and disinherited of the cities, became commonplace. And it was just this interest

of the secure world in the nether world that served as the prototype of muckraking.

All this concern with news, interviews, exposure, and human interest set a premium on the good reporter and reduced the importance of editorial writing and the editorial page. As early as 1871 a writer on journalism observed: "For the majority of readers it is the reporter, not the editor, who is the ruling genius of the newspaper." The old editors of the pre-Civil War era had put a great deal of stock in themselves as makers of opinion through their editorial columns. Now their successors began to realize that their influence on the public mind, such as it was, came from their treatment of the news, not from editorial writing. But getting the news, especially when it came to exposés and human-interest stories, was the reporter's business. Bold reportorial initiative, good reportorial writing, were now very much in demand. In the period from 1870 to about 1890 the salaries of reporters doubled. Better-educated men were more attracted to the profession and were more acceptable in it. Editors who had scorned college graduates began to look for them. The Spanish-American War, a triumph of the new journalism, was nowhere fought more brilliantly than in the columns of the newspapers, and it was covered by a battery of reporters numerous enough and well enough equipped to be used in emergency as military reinforcements. As the reporter's job rose in status, even in glamour, more and more young men with serious literary aspirations were attracted to it as a provisional way of earning a living. These men brought to the journalistic life some of the ideals, the larger interests, and the sense of public responsibility of men of culture.

Finally, the occupational situation of

the reporter was uniquely illuminating. It was not merely that reporters saw and heard things, got the inside story; they sat at the crossroads between the coarse realities of their reportorial beats and the high abstractions and elevated moral tone of the editorial page. Reporters saw what fine things the newspapers said about public responsibility, and they also saw the gross things newspaper managers did to get news or advertising. As Theodore Dreiser, then a young reporter, recalled, they became alert to hypocrisy, perhaps a little cynical themselves, but fundamentally enlightened about the immense gaps between the lofty ideals and public professions of the editorial page and the dirty realities of the business office and the newsroom. And it was into this gap that the muckraking mind rushed with all its fact-finding zeal.

It was, of course, the popular magazine, not the daily newspaper, that stood in the forefront of muckraking, but the muckraking periodicals were profoundly affected by newspaper journalism. The old, respectable magazines, the *Atlantic*, *Harper's*, the *Century*, and *Scribner's*, had been genteel, sedate enterprises selling at thirty-five cents a copy and reaching limited audiences of about 130,000. These periodicals were run by literary men; implicit in their contents was the notion that the magazine is a book in periodical form; they were managed by the conservative publishing houses. The new magazines that emerged at the turn of the century sold at ten or twelve or fifteen cents a copy and reached audiences of from 400,000 to 1,000,000. Their publishers were not literary men but business promoters; their editors were usually former newspaper editors, and they ran a good deal of news copy written by reporters. These magazines, by contrast, were newspapers in periodical form;

they took many of their ideas from daily journalism or the Sunday supplements. They contained not only literature but features that resembled news. And like the daily press they soon began to make news and to become a political force in their own right.

As businessmen, the publishers of these magazines, Frank Munsey, S. S. McClure, John Brisben Walker, and others, resembled their promotion-minded forerunners in daily journalism like E. W. Scripps, Joseph Pulitzer, and William Randolph Hearst. Muckraking for them was the most successful of the circulation-building devices they used. Neither the muckraking publishers and editors nor the muckraking reporters set out to expose evils or to reform society. Although the experience of the *Ladies' Home Journal*, *Munsey's*, and the *Saturday Evening Post* showed that immense circulations could be achieved without ever entering in any serious sense upon it, muckraking was a by-product, perhaps an inevitable one, of the development of mass magazines. Even *McClure's*, the magazine that touched off the movement, had already built a large circulation upon an enterprising use of popular fiction and upon Ida Tarbell's series on the lives of Napoleon and Lincoln. The so-called "muckraking" magazines themselves devoted only a small proportion of their total space to muckraking articles. Only after exposure had proved its popularity did other magazines, notably *Hampton's*, boom their circulations by focusing on muckraking.

A significant illustration of the accidental sources of muckraking was Miss Tarbell's famous series on Standard Oil. S. S. McClure was running, during the late 1890's, a series of articles which he describes in his autobiography as dedicated to "the greatest American business achievements." He had observed that the "feeling of the common people [about the trusts] had a sort of menace in it; they took a threatening attitude toward the Trusts, and without much knowledge." He and his editors decided that a study of Standard Oil, the greatest of the trusts, would have some educational value, and they called in Ida Tarbell, who "had lived for years in the heart of the oil region of Pennsylvania, and had seen the marvelous development of the Standard Oil Trust at first hand." It happened also that Miss Tarbell, whose family had suffered the common disastrous fate of the independent oil-producers, had a great feeling for them. The methods that had been used by Standard Oil were altogether too vulnerable to be played down, and although she hoped her inquiry "might be received as a legitimate historical study . . . to my chagrin I found myself included in a new school, that of the muckrakers." She decided that she would have done with the whole business and seems to have resented the demand of some of her following that she go on with the work of exposure — "I soon found that most of them wanted attacks. They had little interest in balanced findings." Later she did some further work in exposing tariff politics, but she afterwards recalled: "My conscience began to trouble me. Was it not as much my business as a reporter to present this [the favorable] side of the picture as to present the other?" "The public was coming to believe," she felt, as a result of all the work of exposure, "that the inevitable result of corporate industrial management was exploitation, neglect, bullying, crushing of labor, that the only hope was in destroying the system." So she began to write about achievements and improvements in business — under the con-

siderable handicap, to be sure, of her muckraking reputation — became a eulogist of business, and eventually wrote an apologetic biography of the industrialist Judge Gary. In her case the impulse that had been expressed by McClure when he first set out to publicize business achievements came full circle.

Most of the other outstanding figures of the muckrake era were simply writers or reporters working on commission and eager to do well what was asked of them. A few, among them Upton Sinclair and Gustavus Myers, were animated by a deep-going dislike of the capitalist order, but most of them were hired into muckraking or directed toward it on the initiative of sales-conscious editors or publishers. Probably the most socially minded and inquisitive of the muckrakers, except for the Socialists, was Lincoln Steffens; but even his muckraking of American cities began more or less accidentally when McClure refused to allow him to take over an editorship without getting out and familiarizing himself with the country. Others were reluctant dragons. Ray Stannard Baker, whose chief desire was to be a novelist, came to *McClure's* as a writer of secret-service stories and of a book celebrating America's prosperity. Before he began muckraking he was writing faintly eulogistic articles on big business and the trusts! It is perhaps a significant token of the way in which memory rearranges facts in the light of myth that many years later, when Louis Filler was writing his study of the muckrakers, Baker could — no doubt sincerely — refer him to these pieces as examples of early muckraking articles. In fact Baker's first muckraking work tended in a far different direction — it showed up abuses in labor-unionism. Thomas Lawson, the author of the popular *Frenzied Finance,* was a bruised speculator with a bitter contempt for popular democracy. David Graham Phillips, who wrote *The Treason of the Senate*, was making large sums writing novels for the *Saturday Evening Post* when Bailey Millard, the editor of the *Cosmopolitan*, talked him into writing the attack on the Senate. Phillips was extremely reluctant at first, insisting that someone else be engaged to "gather the facts," and agreed to undertake the work only when Gustavus Myers, the Socialist writer, was hired to do the research. Once engaged upon the task, however, he developed a real interest in it.

If, from the standpoint of the editors and journalists themselves, the beginning of muckraking seemed to be more or less "accidental," its ending did not. The large magazine built on muckraking was vulnerable as a business organization. The publishing firm was so large an enterprise and sold its product for so little that it became intensely dependent upon advertising and credit, and hence vulnerable to pressure from the business community. Advertisers did not hesitate to withdraw orders for space when their own interests or related interests were touched upon. Bankers adopted a discriminatory credit policy, so that modest loans could not be secured even for the maintenance of a business of great value and proved stability. In one case, that of *Hampton's*, even espionage was employed to destroy the magazine. One magazine, *Pearson's*, continued to muckrake after 1912, when all the others had fallen into new hands or changed their policies, and its vitality, sustained down to the time of the first World War, has been cited as evidence that muckraking sentiment did not die a spontaneous death, but was choked off at its sources by those who were most affected by its exposures. This is a suggestive, but to my mind not a conclusive, point. It is

conceivable that there may have been enough muckraking sentiment left to support one well-run periodical with a large circulation, but not a half-dozen plus a large number of smaller imitators. Certainly business was hostile and made its hostility felt, but it also seems that the muckraking mood was tapering off. By 1912 it had been raging at a high pitch for nine years. To imagine that it could have gone on indefinitely is to mistake its character.

Consider who the muckrakers were, what their intentions were, and what it was they were doing. Their criticisms of American society were, in their utmost reaches, very searching and radical, but they were themselves moderate men who intended to propose no radical remedies. From the beginning, then, they were limited by the disparity between the boldness of their means and the tameness of their ends. They were working at a time of widespread prosperity, and their chief appeal was not to desperate social needs but to mass sentiments of responsibility, indignation, and guilt. Hardly anyone intended that these sentiments should result in action drastic enough to transform American society. In truth, that society was getting along reasonably well, and the muckrakers themselves were quite aware of it. The group of leading muckrakers that left *McClure's* in 1906 to form the *American Magazine*, as Ray Stannard Baker recalled, was "far more eager to understand and make sure than to dream of utopias. . . . We 'muckraked' not because we hated our world but because we loved it. We were not hopeless, we were not cynical, we were not bitter." Their first announcement promised "the most stirring and delightful monthly book of fiction, humor, sentiment, and joyous reading that is anywhere published. It will reflect a happy, struggling, fighting world, in which, as we believe, good people are coming out on top. . . . Our magazine will be wholesome, hopeful, stimulating, uplifting. . . ."

Finally, it is perhaps necessary to point out that within the limited framework of the reforms that were possible without structural alterations in the American social and economic system, the muckrakers did accomplish something in the form of legislative changes and social face-washing. They enjoyed, after all, some sense of real achievement. Presumably the temper of the early writers for *McClure's* was far more akin to that of the majority of their middle-class audience than was the attitude of the Socialist muckrakers like Gustavus Myers, Upton Sinclair, and Charles Edward Russell, who wanted to push the implications of muckraking discoveries to their utmost practical conclusions. . . .

REALITY AND RESPONSIBILITY

An excellent illustration of the spirit of Progressivism as it manifested itself in the new popular literature is provided by a famous editorial by S. S. McClure in the January 1903 issue of *McClure's*. In this editorial McClure stood back and took a fresh look at his publication and suddenly realized what it was that he and his writers were doing. He observed that his current issue, which was running an article muckraking Minneapolis by Lincoln Steffens, another on Standard Oil by Ida Tarbell, and still another by Ray Stannard Baker on labor, showed a striking and completely unplanned convergence upon a central fact in American life: a general disrespect for law on the part of capitalists, workingmen, politicians, and citizens. Who, he asked, was left in the community to uphold the law? The lawyers? Some of the best of them made a living from advising business firms to evade it. The judges? Among

too many of them the respect for law took the form of respect for quibbles by which they restored to liberty men who on the evidence of common sense would be convicted of malfeasances. The churches? "We know of one, an ancient and wealthy establishment, which had to be compelled by a Tammany hold-over health officer to put its tenements in sanitary condition." "The colleges? They do not understand." "There is no one left," concluded McClure, "none but all of us. . . . We all are doing our worst and making the public pay. The public is the people. We forget that we all are the people. . . . We have to pay in the end, every one of us."

The chief themes of the muckraking magazines are stated here. First is the progressive view of reality — evil-doing among the most respectable people is seen as the "real" character of American life; corruption is found on every side. Second is the idea that the mischief can be interpreted simply as a widespread breaking of the law. I have remarked that Anglo-Saxon thinking emphasized governance by legal rules, as opposed to the widespread tendency among immigrants to interpret political reality in the light of personal relations. If the laws are the right laws, and if they can be enforced by the right men, the Progressive believed, everything would be better. He had a great and abiding faith in the appeal to such abstractions as the law and patriotism, and the efficacy of continued exhortation. Third, there was the appeal to universal personal responsibility and the imputation of personal guilt. . . .

One is impressed, in a review of the literature, with the enormous amount of self-accusation among Progressives. William Allen White saw it when he attributed much of the movement to the fact that "in the soul of the people there is a conviction of their past unrighteousness." The moral indignation of the age was by no means directed entirely against others; it was in a great and critical measure directed inward. Contemporaries who spoke of the movement as an affair of the conscience were not mistaken. Lincoln Steffens had the key to this sense of personal involvement when he entitled his famous muckraking volume *The Shame of the Cities.*

Nothing, indeed, illustrates better than the Introduction to Steffens' volume the fashion in which the Yankee ethos of responsibility had become transmuted into a sense of guilt. Again and again Steffens laid the responsibility for the ugly state of affairs portrayed in his book at the doorsteps of his own readers. "The misgovernment of the American people," he declared, "is misgovernment by the American people. . . . Are the people honest? Are the people better than Tammany?. . . . Isn't our corrupt government, after all, representative?. . . . There is no essential difference between the pull that gets your wife into society or for your book a favorable review, and that which gets a heeler into office, a thief out of jail, and a rich man's son on the board of directors of a corporation. . . . The boss is not a political, he is an American institution, the product of a freed people that have not the spirit to be free. . . . We are responsible, not our leaders, since we follow them. . . . The spirit of graft and of lawlessness is the American spirit. . . . The people are not innocent. That is the only 'news' in all the journalism of these articles. . . . My purpose was . . . to see if the shameful facts, spread out in all their shame, would not burn through our civic shamelessness and set fire to American pride." Steffens closed his introduction by dedicating his book "to the accused — to all the citizens of all the cities in the United States."

It may seem that there was remark-able boldness in this accusatory procedure, but such appearances are often deceptive. Steffens had good reason to know that the substantial American citizen accepted such accusation as valid. The people of Minneapolis and St. Louis had written not in resentment but in encouragement after his exposure of those cities had been published in *McClure's,* and — still more significant — hundreds of invitations poured in from citizens, as individuals or in organized groups, of many other cities inviting exposure on their own premises: "come and show us up; we're worse than they are."

Steffens's argument that it was the people, and particularly the "best" people, who were responsible for corruption cannot be taken, however, as an ultimate comment on human nature or the human condition. He was not preaching universal sinfulness as a token of the fact that most men would be damned, but because he hoped and expected that all could be saved — saved through this ardent appeal to their pride. This is the real function of the pervasively ugly character of reality that the Progressives so frequently harped on: pervasive as it was, it was neither impenetrable nor irremovable: it was an instrument of exhortation, not a clue to life but a fulcrum for reform. Steffens hoped, at bottom, "that our shamelessness is superficial, that beneath it lies a pride which, being real, may save us yet." For when the chips were down he could not but believe, as he said of the situation in St. Louis, that "the people are sound."

Among some reformers this ethos of responsibility to which Steffens appealed simply took the form of an effort to participate in what the rhetoric of the time called "the race life" — which meant, by and large, to get nearer to those who suffered in a more profound and poig-

nant way from the burdens of "reality."
As early as 1892 Jane Addams had delivered a fine, penetrating lecture on "The
Subjective Necessity for Social Settlements," in which she explained how the
sheltered and well-brought-up young
Americans of her generation, reared on
the ideal of social justice and on Protestant moral imperatives, had grown un-
comfortable about their own sincerity,
troubled about their uselessness, and
restless about being "shut off from the
common labor by which they live and
which is a great source of moral and
physical health." Similarly a character
in one of the social novels of H. H. Boye-
sen, the son of a rich contractor, pro-
fessed "a sneaking sense of guilt when
I am too comfortable," and left high
society to plunge into what he called
'the great discordant tumultuous life,
with its passions and cries of distress."
Characters with the same motivation
were constantly to be found in the pages
of *McClure's* — now, however, no longer
only as the protagonists of fiction, but as
the authors of articles. Where this impulse was translated into action it sent
a host of earnest reformers into the field
to engage themselves in various useful
philanthropies. But on the purely verbal
level, where of necessity it had to remain
for most people, it resulted on occasion
in a rather strenuous moral purgation,
not unlike the pathetic proletarianism
that swept over many American intellec-
uals in the 1930's. One Florence Wilkin-
on contributed to *McClure's* a poem en-
itled "The Tortured Millions":

. . . They are dying that I may live, the
  tortured millions,
By the Ohio River, the Euphrates, the Rhone.
They wring from the rocks my gold, the
  tortured millions;
Sleepless all night they mix my daily bread;
With heavy feet they are trampling out my
  vintage;

They go to a hungry grave that I may be
  fed. . . .
I warm my hands at the fires of ruining
  houses;
On a dying mother's breast I sink my head;
Last night my feet were faint from idleness,
I bathed my feet in blood her children shed.
O thou eternal Law, I wish this not to be.
Nay, raise them from the dust and punish me.

So the middle-class citizen received
quite earnestly the exhortations that
charged him with personal responsibility
for all kinds of social ills. It was his business to do something about them. Indeed, he must do something if he was
ever to feel better. But what should he
do? He was too substantial a fellow to
want to make any basic changes in a
society in which he was so typically a
prosperous and respectable figure. What
he needed, therefore, was a feeling that
action was taking place, a sense that the
moral tone of things was being improved
and that he had a part in this improvement. Corruption thus became a particularly fine issue for the moral energies
of the Progressive. He was ready to be
convinced that the country was thoroughly wicked, and the muckrakers supplied him with a wealth of plausible
evidence.

In time the muckraking and reform
writers seem to have become half-con-
scious of the important psychic function
their work was performing for themselves
and their public, quite apart from any
legislative consequences or material
gains. They began to say, in effect, that
even when they were unable to do very
much to change the exercise of political
power, they liked the sense of effort and
the feeling that the moral tone of political life had changed. "It is not the material aspect of this," they began to say,
"but the moral aspect that interests us."
William Allen White dated the begin-
nings of this shift from "materialism" to

"moral values" from the war with Spain when "the spirit of sacrifice overcame the spirit of commercialism," and the people saw "that if we could learn to sacrifice our own interests for those of a weaker people, we would learn the lesson needed to solve the great problem of democracy — to check our national greed and to make business honest." McClure himself gave characteristic expression to this high valuation of the intangibles when he praised Charles Evans Hughes's exposure of the New York life-insurance companies for the enormous "tonic effect of the inquiry," which, he felt, had very likely saved thousands of young men from making compromises with honor. They saw that "public disgrace" awaited evildoers, and "there is no punishment so terrible as public disclosure of evil doing." Related to this emphasis on moral as opposed to material values was a fresh assertion of disdain for money and monetary success, very reminiscent of the disdain of the Mugwump type for the materialists. With this came a disparagement of material achievement. San Francisco, remarked George Kennan, was a successful and prosperous city, but it had put stress "upon material achievement and business prosperity rather than

upon civic virtue and moral integrity. But what shall it profit a city if it gain the whole world and lose its own soul?" Probably no statesman of the time had a better intuitive understanding of the interest of the reform mind in moral intangibles than Theodore Roosevelt, whose preachments exploited it to the full. And no observer had a better insight into T. R.'s relation to his time than the Sage of Emporia, who declared quite properly that "Roosevelt's power in this land is a spiritual power. His is not a kingdom of this earth. . . . It is immaterial whether or not the Supreme Court sustains him in his position on the rate bill, the income tax, the license for corporations, or the inheritance tax; not for the establishment of a system of statutes was he born into this world; but rather like all great teachers, that by his life and his works he should bear witness unto the truth." This was a penetrating comment upon the meaning of the reform literature as a kind of symbolic action. For, besides such material accomplishment as they had to show for themselves, the Progressive writers could claim that they had provided a large part of the American people with a necessary and (as they would have said) wholesome catharsis.

David Chalmers: THE CELESTIAL CROWN

In The Social and Political Ideas of the Muckrakers *David Chalmers focuses upon the positive accomplishments of the muckraking crusade. Chalmers sees a common thread that unified the muckrakers in their approach to American social conditions.*

From David M. Chalmers, *The Social and Political Ideas of the Muckrakers* (New York, 1964), pp. 104–116. Reprinted by permission of the Citadel Press.

LINCOLN STEFFENS told in his autobiography of accepting a challenge
to prove that his home town of Green-
wich, Connecticut, was typically corrupt. While he spoke, his assistant,
Walter Lippmann, drew on a blackboard
a diagram of the dishonest functioning
of government in the average American
city. Then with the help of the audience,
Steffens filled in the names of the Green-
wich exemplars. According to the traditional depiction of them, the muckrakers functioned like this, writing in the
names of grafters on a ready-made chart.
This interpretation, however, misses the
real spirit and importance of the movement. The difficulty in understanding
the muckrakers results from the nature
of their crusade and the way it developed. The participants were journalists,
not academicians or legislators. Their
work was adapted to the medium of the
popular magazines and tended to develop in installment fashion. Few of the
writers initially began with a broad analysis of the national ills. They started
with a particular city or industry and
built up a picture of the nation as a
whole, article by article, series by series.
Each crystalized his philosophy before
the end of the era of exposés. Nevertheless, the readers' initial impression of
naiveté and lack of direction was often
the one that remained.

Theodore Roosevelt's label of "muckrakers" entrenched this popular reaction
by creating a simplified picture of aim-
less and often unjustified sensationalism.
Though the people read and absorbed
the message of these journalists, the stere-
otype stuck. But the effect of the President's phrase was not only upon the general public but also the writers themselves. Although Charles Edward Russell,
Upton Sinclair, Thomas Lawson, and
Alfred Henry Lewis gloried in the title,
David Graham Phillips and Ida Tarbell
were extremely upset, and Phillips soon
gave up the magazines in order to concentrate on his novels. Some writers seem
partially to have accepted T.R.'s criticism. The time came soon afterwards
when Lincoln Steffens announced that
he was done with exposés. "Now solutions," he proclaimed, although he had
been so engaged all along.

The fact that the movement was educational, rather than legislative, adds an
additional difficulty to understanding the
era. The journalists, agreeing upon a
common enemy, wished specific reforms
and often whole programs of correction,
but most of them did not feel that they
were in a position to lead a political
movement. Rather, they set themselves
to creating an informed public opinion
that would make progress possible.

The muckrakers were not intent on
keeping aloof from political affairs.
Charles Edward Russell and Upton Sinclair were hardy campaigners on the
Socialist ticket. G. K. Turner testified in
crime and vice investigations. Ray Stannard Baker soon gave up his anti-politi-
cal ideas, took part in local politics in
Michigan, and later became a campaign
adviser to Robert M. La Follette. Lincoln
Steffens was involved in practically every
stirring of municipal and state reform.

There can be little doubt of the journalists' earnestness and sense of dedication. Russell's muckrake convictions led
him to join the Socialist Party. The letters and diaries of Lincoln Steffens, Ida
Tarbell, Ray Stannard Baker, and David
Graham Phillips showed how their hopes
for the good which they might do became the central force in their lives. Although this ego-involvement was responsible for Thomas Lawson's flights of
fancy, for the others it meant that their
effectiveness depended on a high stan-

dard of honesty and integrity. This feeling was demonstrated when the top writers on *McClure's* resigned rather than be a party to S. S. McClure's speculative experiments.

But much more was involved in the movement than the seriousness of its participants. The muckrakers presented affirmative creeds, ranging from G. K. Turner's belief that big business should be released from the trammels of laws designed for a bygone competitive economy, to the socialism of Upton Sinclair and Charles Edward Russell. All of the writers realised that vast changes had taken place in the land. More than any other group they made the people aware of what twentieth-century America was like. Quickly passing over the fields which had concerned previous generations of reformers, they evidenced little interest in currency or civil service improvements. Although they all attacked the tariff, only Ida Tarbell believed that it was a vital national problem. For the belated nineteenth-century answer to the growth of monopoly, the Sherman Anti-Trust Act, there was only minority support.

Despite the diversity of their remedial views, all of the muckrakers laid the evils of society to the rise of new economic conditions. The journalists used a variety of terms: the "interests," "the System," high or frenzied finance, plutocracy, industrial aristocracy, the trusts and monopoly. In one way or another the writers were talking about the same thing. The specific agent in the national orgy of corruption was the corporations. Their highest utility, Ray Stannard Baker wrote, was that they enabled "reputable people to participate in the profits of disreputable business enterprises without disturbing their moral complacency." It was just this popular

indifference and acquiescence that the muckrakers tried to upset. They attempted to educate the people to the realization, as Will Irwin stated it, that "the crime of stealing the means of production through corrupt legislatures and corrupt market manipulations is as great and heinous, doubtless, as the crime of stealing silver spoons from the safe of a wealthy burgher." The fault was not in the corporate form itself but rather the use to which it was being put. The moral development of the nation failed to keep pace with an enormous material expansion. The profit motive, they pointed out, had been enthroned in America. They all believed that "Business" had become the ruling force in society and, with the exception of G. K. Turner, they did not like the results. Lincoln Steffens summed it up when he wrote that "Business, the mere machinery of living, has become in America the purpose of life, the end to which all other goods — honour, religion, politics, men, women and children, the very nation itself — are sacrificed."

Muckraking then, despite its gaudy show of accusations, was not directed toward seeking out individuals as scapegoats. The emphasis on prominent men as exemplification of evil was a matter of journalistic style rather than ideology. Although the muckrakers were concerned with the need for leadership, it rarely approached becoming a cult. Only Lincoln Steffens and Thomas Lawson seriously relied upon a theory of leadership. Lawson's messiah was himself, while Steffens looked to the outstanding men of business and politics to arouse a general sense of dedication to public service.

The disinclination of the journalists to tie their movement to the political chariot of any particular man in public life emerged clearly from the body of their writing. To most of them, Theodore Roosevelt initially promised the best chance for a great national readjustment. Alfred Henry Lewis and Will Irwin never faltered in their admiration, but the others became disillusioned with the President. His friends, Ray Stannard Baker and Lincoln Steffens, who held the highest hopes for him, were the most disappointed. He was, they came to believe, unconcerned about economic problems and hopelessly a trimmer. By the time most of the writers crystalized their ideas, they discovered that the Rough Rider from Oyster Bay had been left behind.

The muckrakers had no greater faith in the political parties than in outstanding individuals. Almost all of them rejected the standard national solutions of replacing the "ins" with the "outs," or "bad" with "good" government. Even the minority of Democrats among the journalists were not willing to claim that a shift in political power would in any way change conditions. Steffens, Lewis, Baker, Russell and Phillips repeatedly wrote that "Business" ruled in both parties. Nevertheless, few of the journalists became radicals. Only Charles Edward Russell was led to socialism during the muckrake era by the conviction that the traditional channels were hopeless. Upton Sinclair was already there before he turned to muckraking. . . .

Despite the growing aggregation of wealth and the inability of the country's institutions to protect the interests of the common man, the muckrakers were not prophets of gloom. All believed that the evils could be corrected and that the moment of crisis was at hand. Only Will Irwin and G. K. Turner felt that no action was necessary. To everyone, except Lawson and perhaps Turner, America meant the promise of a freer and more equalitarian land. They saw the story of the nation's march toward that goal as a dialectic process by which every struggle against a newly rising wave of reaction resulted in a new advance for the people. Both Baker and Phillips wrote of such waves, and Russell and Sinclair saw in their own times a repetition of the pre-Civil War unrest. As homemade evolutionists and environmentalists, even when they were not economic determinists, they accepted this as the path to progress. . . .

The writers of magazine exposés were basically moderates in most fields. They spoke as representatives of the middle classes of the nation's cities and towns. It would be difficult to apply Richard Hofstadter's thesis in *The Age of Reform* to the muckrakers and maintain that they were led to reform as members of the old middle class which was being shaded by the rise of the trusts and the great fortunes. The muckrakers, perhaps apart from their class confreres, were at the peak of their professional power and mobility. On the whole, they came to the Progressive movement through the discovery of national corruption, rather than by conscious or unconscious comparison of their class or status position. As a group, they looked neither backward to an intensely democratic small America nor forward to a highly centralized nationalistic state. With the exception of Charles Edward Russell, they did not understand or attach any great importance to the agrarian unrest of the previous decades. Nor did they preach a doctrine of class warfare. There were stirrings of the latter phenomenon in the writings of Baker, Phillips, Russell, and Sinclair, but even they saw class conflict as a peaceful force working within the democratic framework. The socialism of Upton Sinclair and Charles Edward

Russell was not extreme and contained only a limited amount of the Marxian paraphernalia. It was primarily a sense of frustration that led Russell into increasing radicalism in the last days before the outbreak of the First World War. In the main, the muckrakers believed that they did not believe that virtue resided solely in any one group in the society. They were for "the public," whose interests, however, always seemed to be typically middle-class.

This is clearly shown in the attitude toward organized labor. Although all of these journalists at one time or another wrote on the subject of unions and the plight of the wage earner, they were usually without conclusions. They merely cautioned against violence and lamented unfair union practices. None saw labor as a counter-balancing group to aggregate wealth in a compromise society. On the other hand, only Burton Hendrick was openly hostile. The sins of labor seemed less menacing than those of capital, and there was much talk of "the public" whose interests had to be protected against both the unions and the trusts.

One theme that was almost completely absent from the writings of the muckrakers was a consideration of "big government." Hendrick alone dealt with it explicitly. He opposed centralized national power, but he did not believe that it threatened to become a reality. When the magazine crusaders pondered the role of the national government, they were concerned only with the privileges which might be given to business. For the most part, the non-socialists believed that the existing type of government would endure if it could be made responsive to the will of an informed people. To this end, the muckrakers offered enlightenment in their columns and called for such reforms as initiative referendum, recall, direct primaries, and the popular election of Senators. One might suppose from the Socialists' talk of public operation for the common good that a super-bureaucracy was in the making. However, they did not discuss this possibility. Although control of the national administration was to affect the revolution, Sinclair talked of his cooperative commonwealth as though it were a series of individual utopian colonies. Russell never dealt with the problem at all.

Probably the outstanding weakness in the philosophy of the muckrakers was their lack of a broad knowledge of economics. Although highlighting many evils, most of them did not understand the workings of the industrial and financial mechanisms. As George Mowry, the leading authority on this era, has pointed out, the Progressives tended to talk in "moral rather than economic terms." This was surely true of the muckrakers. Whether or not it was a substitute for the middle-class absence of a consciousness of class consciousness, they placed great emphasis upon the role of public spirited altruism. However, if their outlook was moralistic because they believed that man could be made "good," the means was to pass laws to change the environment and conditions which made men "bad."

The strong point in the ideas of Samuel Hopkins Adams and Tom Lawson was their realization that there was much about the industrial machine which could not be controlled by public opinion and moral pressure. Having a better understanding of the financial organization of business, they explained why over-capitalization forced higher prices on the American consuming public. The muckrake-Socialists had the most detailed con ception of how the economic mechanism worked. Charles Edward Russell cogently connected public buying power with industrial health, and he explained how over-capitalization and the drive for profits forced business to act in a way inimical to its own interests. The malignant force of "the surplus" held a central role in the analyses of Russell and Upton Sinclair. Their apocalyptic brand of economics, however, had the faults of its virtues. There is perhaps something depressing and pessimistic about a social process — even when working toward the best of ends — which is not amenable to the control or direction of the men whom it is supposed to aid.

Most of the muckrakers were not looking backward. Perhaps, a few exponents of an anti-trust, competitive America thought longingly of the days gone by. The vast majority of the others would have agreed with Lincoln Steffens when he attacked those who mistakenly believed that the nation could turn back the pages of history to the days of Thomas Jefferson or Andrew Jackson. Will Irwin, who felt that the existing institutions were satisfactory, maintained that competition would work because it would adjust the new industrialism to the service of the common people. Steffens, Phillips, and Baker, as well as the muckrake-Socialists, were convinced that the forces of evolution were at work in human society. The Socialists saw a future of increasing progress and believed that trusts were an inevitable step in the movement toward a cooperative commonwealth. Others lauded the new industrialism and the good that might result from its enormous output. G. K. Turner, declining to blame big business for corruption, felt that it was bringing order to a chaotic competitive world. David Graham Phillips wrote the most

enthusiastic message of praise in *The Reign of Gilt*. America, he explained proudly, was being emancipated by the machine. By raising the nation's standard of living, industry was working like science and education to break down prejudice and ignorance. By contributing to a new political fluidity, it would bring the end of the bosses and plutocracy.

Most of the journalists searched for hopeful signs of the growing productivity being applied to the service of the community. Burton Hendrick hailed the workers' villages of Gary, as well as the Carnegie and Rockefeller foundations, although the rest of the muckrakers strongly opposed anything that had the appearance of philanthropy or charity. Ida Tarbell was quick to seize upon the first encouraging instances of public-spiritedness on the part of the titans of industry. Steffens, with his interests in the techniques of leadership, relied upon the outstanding men of politics and business to bring the mass of citizens to a higher sense of community service. Many of the writers praised the scientific management theories of F. W. Taylor. Upton Sinclair alone raised a discordant note by demanding to know exactly how the greater profits were to be divided.

Although concentrating on the central problems of society, the crusading journalists sought a more complete democracy in all parts of American life. Together with Russell, Tarbell, Baker and Sinclair, Phillips examined the role of the woman in the partnerships of marriage and national affairs. Turner and Steffens found the city a unique opportunity for experimentation in progressive democracy. As a group, the muckrakers had no agrarian prejudice against city or immigrant, even though there were strong strains of love for the land and nostalgia for the small town in the writing of Baker and Phillips. Upton Sinclair alone displayed hatred for the life of the metropolis which he equated with plutocratic consumption and exploitation of the immigrant.

It would be difficult to maintain that the muckrakers followed at least some of their Progressive brethren along the paths of racism or Anglo-Saxon bias. Will Irwin was a little gullible on the subject of the Negro, but his failure to arrive at any solution to the West Coast prejudice was not based upon a belief in racial or cultural inferiority of the Oriental. Ray Stannard Baker's abandonment of his strident advocacy of Negro equalitarianism was in reality a retreat from socialism. Although he came to recommend a slower path, he did not give up his opposition to second-class citizenship for the Negro. Phillips and Russell were strongly critical of English society. Hendrick followed the liberal anthropology of Franz Boas in explaining varying ethnic stocks in terms of the plasticity of man responding to differences in environment. Lincoln Steffens, in writing of corruption in Philadelphia and Rhode Island, maintained that corrupt government was not ethnic, but American. Phillips hailed the immigrant as a strong force against aristocracy and tyranny. All of the muckrakers believed, with Charles Edward Russell, that any action which denied the "normal ties of sympathy and goodwill between men" exacted a cost too great for any nation to bear.

The wielders of the muckrake exposed corruption in order that it might be corrected. Their analysis of national life probed deeply into the vast changes that had taken place during the previous half-century. Collectively they presented one of the first comprehensive description of the business civilization that had become the ideal and the motive force of the American nation. With their criticism the muckrakers helped lay the groundwork of public concern which resulted in many of the reforms of the next half century. In addition, these journalists had positive reform views to express and were able to do so in the popular magazines for more than a decade. They explained that the corruption which had become general in American life resulted from the privileges sought and obtained by the giant business enterprises that had emerged in the United States after the Civil War. The muckrakers did not reject the new industrialism and the dominant corporate form, but rather insisted that both be used for the public good.

The best illustration of the nature of the muckrakers' message can be found in a letter which Lincoln Steffens wrote to Theodore Roosevelt in the spring of 1907:

I am not seeking proof of crime and dishonesty. . . . What I am after is the cause and the purpose and the methods by which our government, city, state and federal, is made to represent not the common, but the special interests; the reason why it is so hard to do right in the U.S.; the secret of the power which makes it necessary for you, Mr. President, to fight to give us a "square deal." In brief, I want to . . . explain why it is that you have to force the Senate to pass a pure food bill or one providing for the regulation of railroads. . . .

And please don't misunderstand me. . . . This is a point on which you, Mr. President, and I have never agreed. . . . I am looking upward to — an American Democracy. You ask men in office to be honest, I ask them to serve the people. . . .

Louis G. Geiger: MUCKRAKING — THEN AND NOW

In his article, "Muckrakers — Then and Now" Professor Louis Geiger argues that the muckrakers failed in the attempt to develop a national synthesis of reform. Professor Geiger probes the sources of that failure and fundamentally locates them in factors independent of the muckrakers' own shortcomings.

THE terms muckraking and muckraker call up for us all an image of a wave of enthusiasm for reform that began more or less with Theodore Roosevelt's arrival at the White House, and abruptly collapsed about the time he left. The almost universal familiarity with the phenomenon, at least in general terms, gives an illusion of a mighty army of writers and magazines reaching into every cranny in the country. In point of fact, of course, the magazine writers who qualified for the term of muckraker and who proudly wore it as their badge numbered scarcely a dozen, and the muckraking magazines which made their work a trademark and claim to circulation were even fewer — it was a Gideon's host.

The muckraking fashion could not have aroused a nation to action, however, had it not been for a thorough earlier conditioning of an audience. Since the 1870s a variety of writers, public men, scholars and agrarians had been developing a pattern of complaint and concern about the results and dislocations of the new age of industrialism. The People's Party had attempted to give it coherent form in the 1890s. It was upon this tradition, and upon the sensitized audience it had developed, that the classic muckrakers built.

They were dependent too for their effectiveness upon a great variety of local agitators who hit out at local grievances and spoke to local audiences. For example, the Claude Wetmore whose name appears along with Lincoln Steffens' as the co-author of "Tweed Days in St. Louis," the first of the "Shame of the Cities" series, was much more than a shadowy local figure attempting to write an account for a magazine and finding it necessary to get assistance from Steffens. Wetmore was, in fact, the crusading city editor of the St. Louis *Post-Dispatch*, who had established muckraking as a style of St. Louis journalism, one that was taken up by three of the four major dailies of the city during the 1890s. St. Louis muckraking was a decade old when Steffens appeared on the scene, and for that matter Joseph W. Folk was well launched before Steffens heard of him. What Steffens had to say — with Wetmore — had all appeared earlier in the St. Louis papers — documentation, style and all. Folk understandably welcomed the additional publicity that *McClure's* could provide, but he was hardly dependent upon it in Missouri, certainly not half as much as he was on the *Post-Dispatch*, the *Republic* and the *Star*. Folk, a lawyer and a politician, was an accomplished muckraker in his own way. No one knew better than he how to slant an interview toward a desired end.

A somewhat comparable situation de-

From Louis G. Geiger, "Muckrakers — Then and Now," *Journalism Quarterly*, Vol. 43, No. 3 (Autumn 1966), pp. 469–476. Reprinted by permission of *Journalism Quarterly* and of the author.

veloped in North Dakota. In the early 1900s a town-rural Progressive movement developed which eventually created a coalition of minority Democrats and discontented Republicans able to elect a progressive Catholic Democrat governor for three successive terms in a state that was overwhelmingly Republican and more than 75 per cent Protestant. Not the least important element in arousing North Dakota voters to action against the "interests" was an oddly named little magazine, the *North Dakota Farmer and Sanitary Home,* run by Edwin Fremont Ladd, a professor of chemistry. Ladd concentrated on food adulteration and false advertising of seed grains and paints. He demonstrated to the satisfaction of a receptive rural audience that cheating was practically the normal practice in the food and supplies business, in purchasing from the producer, and in sales to the consumer. The People's Party and the Alliance had earlier established the conviction that the elevator companies and the railroads were cheats. There is little doubt that in North Dakota it was Ladd, not Lawson, nor Baker, nor Steffens, nor Sinclair, who spoke effectively to the public. And it was Ladd more than Harvey Wiley or Samuel Hopkins Adams who turned Senator Porter McCumber, a conservative Republican, into a supporter of pure food and drug legislation long before TR was.

These examples at least suggest that it is somewhat easier to demonstrate that muckraking in the national magazines coincided with the development of a national atmosphere of reform than it is to measure the extent of any cause-effect relationship between magazine muckraking and the rise of reform sentiment, particularly in agrarian America. Whatever influence the national magazines

had in Missouri and North Dakota was related to the local preparation of an audience. Moreover, it is doubtful that the muckrakers reached people in rural communities at all, or even a great many in towns under 10,000, which is to say more than half the population of the country. Farmers had just got Rural Free Delivery in 1896, and by 1906 they were just becoming accustomed to the luxury of a daily city newspaper. Their magazines were farm journals. As late as the 1920s one would not find many city-style magazines in farm homes. Nor is it likely that the muckrakers reached a significant portion of the laboring population in the cities, except indirectly. It has been estimated that the muckraking journals' total circulation came to about 3 million copies per month at its peak, about that of the *Saturday Evening Post* in the late 1920s, or one copy for about every seven families. This is a substantial number, to be sure, even allowing for what must have been numerous duplicate subscriptions, but it really represents a considerable saturation in some areas and a complete miss in others.

Missing the agrarians was serious, for more than any other single group they had influenced the formation of a sort of national consensus of what the major problems of a transitional America were, as well as a formula for their solution; a central theme was the determination to call in the Federal Government to act positively in the national interest. The trouble with the consensus was that it had definite limitations for the agrarians, and these the muckrakers could never succeed in modifying enough to create a truly national reform synthesis. The agrarian orientation was particularly important because of its influence in Congress. Here the really effective and consistent Progressives were a coalition of

Bryanite Democrats and insurgent Republicans from the South and West. Even the standpatters from these regions responded more than a little to the agrarian reform conditioning.

We must assess the impact of the muckrakers, therefore, in terms of their reaching not much further than the urban middle class. Here they had their major effect, for this audience had been deaf to the appeals of the Populists and Bryanites. The muckrakers restated the traditional concerns that had been developed by the agrarians in terms that were more sophisticated and less personally or class oriented than the agrarians had done. 'In addition, the muckrakers changed the tone and the direction of their attack. Shrill though they could be on occasion, they usually avoided the rural invective, and they employed none of the country vs. city terminology that featured and marred the agrarians' earlier reform attempts on the national level. The muckrakers were reformist, but often sympathetic and understanding, even of those they attacked; they had none of the sound of revolution that could creep into Populist rhetoric. The muckrakers expanded the definitions of national problems and the remedies for them; they added problems peculiar to the city, that had hitherto been considered purely local, even by city folk themselves. They attempted also, although with indifferent success, to revive once more as national concerns such questions as the white man's mistreatment of the Negro; like the city, the Negro had been consigned to the care of the area where he lived.

A significant feature of the muckrakers' approach was their appeal to the middle-class conscience; here they touched the nerve of a growing sense of guilt, which was being aroused as well as demonstrated by such practitioners of good works as the settlement workers. The muckrakers offered a way for all to act; not all were able nor willing to go to the slums, but all could be concerned, and all could strike at least some small blow in the cause of good government. The muckrakers' message was plain: the responsibility for what was wrong lay in the indifference of the citizen himself; everyone was cheating in a society based on cheating. Nevertheless, moral regeneration was within the reach of all.

It was the broadened, urbanized language of reform, the addition of new questions without ignoring the old, although refining and universalizing them, which defined the agrarian-middle class coalition, albeit a temporary one, which would be known as Progressivism. From the urban side a real synthesis may have been possible, owing to the nature of muckraking education, but from the rural side, which the muckrakers did not reach, it was not. The agrarians never accepted the problems of the city as their own, nor did they accept society's sins as theirs. These, in the agrarians' eyes, were the cities', the robber barons', the railroads', the money-lenders', or what not. From the beginning, therefore, the apparent Progressive synthesis was only a military alliance, at least from one side, and was almost certain to collapse when one party was satisfied, or when the alliance was put to any serious strain.

The absence of a true synthesis can be demonstrated, I think, again in North Dakota and Missouri, in the composition and behavior of the Progressive coalition in Congress, and in the general nature of the so-called Progressive program that was enacted into federal law or placed in the Constitution. In North Dakota, Progressivism was never better than a temporary expedient between two waves of

Populist-agrarian reformism. The local inadequacy of a successful Progressive regime that lasted six years was demonstrated by the sudden rise of the Nonpartisan League, a socialist-populist movement more to the liking of agrarians than the synthetic rural-urban alliance had been.

In Missouri, the St. Louis and Kansas City newspapers aroused the countryside for Folk, a Democrat city lawyer backed by Republican businessmen of St. Louis, in a campaign to take over the state house. For a time, Folk managed a true reform synthesis; he made a determined effort to face the problems of St. Louis and Kansas City government, as well as to please his agrarian constituents. Within four years, however, his coalition of country Democrats and city Republicans was showing signs of weakness, and in eight it had collapsed, in part at least because rural Democrats would not regard urban problems as their own.

It took local muckraking activity, and a newspaper press that got out to country readers, for any sort of real urban-rural reform combination to be effected. In Missouri, the connection was made, but we have a good illustration here of the limited span of agrarians' interest in urban problems, even with vigorous local papers and a dynamic public leader to keep it alive. In North Dakota, the most rural state in the nation, the urban side of reformism was meaningless even on the local level. Urban reformism did make headway in the heavily populated states in the East, as state-wide movements, to be sure, but party structure in the East, middle-class distrust of the agrarians, and the situation in Congress worked against any possibility that eastern legislators might construct a national reformist coalition.

In Washington, the most vigorous and imaginative of the reform leaders — La Follette, Norris, Gronna, Dolliver, Tillman, Beveridge — all came from regions where the agrarians' influence was strong. Not until around 1910 did the Eastern states begin sending any substantial support to represent the urban middle-class side of Progressivism; these representatives came chiefly as Democrats who had overturned conservative Republicans. Coming late, and being a minority, they served mainly to shift the balance of power toward the insurgent Bryanite agrarians, who also enjoyed an added advantage of over-apportionment. Roosevelt and Wilson, both of whom would develop their own theories of reform, had to depend upon the agrarians for their programs; indeed, not infrequently the Presidents were carried along further than they personally intended to go. Undoubtedly many Western and Southern Congressmen read the muckrakers, even if their constituents did not, and were the better informed for it. But they were not likely to venture too far beyond their constituents' firmly established tradition of what the national problems were, nor to argue too much with the agrarians' view that the city was essentially an alien America whose problems were the concern of those foolish enough to live in them.

As final testimony in evidence of the incompleteness of the muckrakers' attempted synthesis of a truly national, all-class reform movement, recall for a moment the major federal legislation and constitutional amendments that come under the label of progressive achievements in the first decade and a half of this century, and recall how many of these were really of agrarian origin. With the exception of the subtreasury scheme and free silver, the Populist-

Bryanite program was almost entirely enacted by 1916, either outright or in spirit. The Federal Land Bank Act, the Smith-Lever farm extension act and the Smith-Hughes vocational teaching act were clearly aimed at redressing grievances of the agrarian interest. Where is there comparable national legislation to deal with the social and urban problems delineated by the muckrakers, such as the growth of city slums, the blight of poverty and unemployment, prostitution, isolation of immigrants or racial minorities? There were some significant beginning steps in the protection of industrial labor, but the stock exchanges went on as before, despite Lawson's lurid allegations. The Negro was actually set back further than he already was by the Wilson administration's employment policies, and he got no new legal or constitutional protections. For the immigrant there was a rising threat of nativism and exclusion.

The effort to create a truly national climate of reform, rather than to rectify special class grievances as the agrarians had proposed, was therefore both the glory of the muckrakers and the point where they failed. The reasons usually given for the muckrakers' failure or rejection, most of them implying something wrong with the muckrakers themselves, are largely guesses or plausible explanations. The charges of exaggeration, of concentration on economic issues, of offering no coherent program, of naive optimism, have become standardized more by repetition than by research. The most concrete explanation, and one that has often been ignored, is Louis Filler's assertion that the muckraking magazines were deliberately put out of business by hostile financial interests which bought up the magazines or withdrew advertising.

The muckrakers were, in fact, a remarkable group of journalists — well-educated, highminded, industrious and conscientious, and above all, themselves personally concerned. They were far above the average of their craft in the quality of their writing and in their conception of journalism as a responsible means of public education. As for the incompleteness or one-sidedness of their analyses and their remedies, we can hardly blame them for not outdoing their contemporaries, or because they did not anticipate sophisticated concepts and information that would be developed by social scientists in the years to come. Nor could they anticipate that the fruits of reform — the welfare state and the affluent society — would produce the very opposite of the personal involvement they sought, that depersonalization would bring misgiving and disillusionment. The muckrakers were not, after all, prophets or professional social scientists. Even if they had known better, they could not have proposed a course of action that went beyond the public willingness to understand or to accept. As for the muckrakers' dishonesty, we can admit that they pointed up their stories, but not that they lied. Ed Butler, boss of St. Louis, a convicted or confessed briber, boodler and perjurer, would be sardonically amused to know that his accusers are now suspected of dishonesty themselves. The muckrakers had to live in their own times, and they had to shout at times to make their middle class audience hear. Whatever they might have done, the circulation limitations of their media, the so-called general national magazines, would have defeated them.

Moreover, the times were not yet really right for the synthesis that the muckrakers were attempting. The agrar-

ian side of the nation was still too powerful and opinionated, and the urban side
still too fragmented as middle class,
ethnic minorities, and the poor to accept
wholesale reformism; indeed, even the
middle class was unprepared for the
urban emphasis offered by the muckrakers. By 1916, the opportunity had
passed; the agrarians were beyond reach,
because most of their traditional reform
program had been enacted into law or
accepted into the Constitution. And the
agrarians were getting even further out
of reach, for they were moving toward
their 1920s preoccupation with parochial,
vocational concerns. The war completed
the separation. The President and the
urban middle class and Southern agrarians on one side and Western agrarians
on the other split over entry into the war,
fell out yet more over its conduct, and
completed their breach over the League.
The muckrakers, for the most part, went
along with the President, and some lent

themselves to whipping up the war
hysteria which victimized particularly
some of the agrarians' most respected
leaders. . . .

In their day the muckrakers, striking
out on a wide front, set out to create a
general climate of reformism, and with
it a broad acceptance of personal responsibility. That they essentially failed was
as much the limitation of their media
and of their audience as it was the muckrakers' error. The muckrakers typified
their own times in their enthusiasm about
the possibilities of solving their problems. Undoubtedly their optimism was
a manifestation of an innocence now
gone. Yet a measure of optimism, if not
of innocence, appears to be an element
essential to all really successful reform
periods in America. It is this very thing
which was missing in the 1920s, which
reappeared during the 1930s, peculiarly
enough, and which eludes us in the 1960s.

Suggestions for Additional Reading

A pioneer work in tracing the history of the muckraking movement is C. C. Regier's *The Era of the Muckrakers* (Chapel Hill, 1932). The book illuminates the muckraking interest in exposing corruption in many aspects of American society, but the interpretations offered are sometimes superficial. Better written and containing many perceptive insights into muckraking is Louis Filler's *Crusaders for American Liberalism* (New York, 1939), now available in paperback edition. Filler's book is an eloquent defense of the movement's contribution to the liberal tradition. A recent study that focuses on several outstanding muckrakers is David Chalmers' *The Social and Political Ideas of the Muckrakers* (New York, 1964).

With a revival of interest in the muckrakers two anthologies of muckraker writings have appeared. The collection edited by Arthur and Lila Weinberg, *The Muckrakers* (New York, 1961), presents well-selected, full-length examples of the muckrakers' approach. More widely inclusive in its selection of materials is the collection edited by Harvey Swados, *Years of Conscience* (Cleveland and New York, 1962). A shortcoming to be noted is that some of the excerpts have been unduly abbreviated.

A characteristic of many reformers of the Progressive period was the tendency to continued self-examination. Several of the muckrakers tried to evaluate their own activities and motives, especially through autobiographies. These books, especially when balanced against the views of contemporaries and later critics, shed invaluable light on the sources of the muckraking mind and upon the Progressive movement generally. Among the various muckrakers' autobiographies the classic is still *The Autobiography of Lincoln Steffens* (New York, 1931), 2 vols. This book traces Steffens' evolution from liberalism to a radicalism that supported the Mexican and Russian revolutions. Very useful for a fuller understanding of Steffens' career is *The Letters of Lincoln Steffens*, edited by Ella Winter and Granville Hicks (New York, 1938). Other muckraker autobiographies include Ida Tarbell's *All in a Day's Work* (New York, 1939), Ray Stannard Baker's *American Chronicle* (New York, 1945) and Charles Edward Russell's *Bare Hands and Stone Walls* (New York, 1933). Excerpts from the Baker and Tarbell autobiographies are found in *The Progressives*, edited by Carl Resek (Indianapolis and New York, 1967). Worth attention is muckraking publisher S. S. McClure's *My Autobiography* (New York, 1914).

Biographic studies of several prominent muckrakers are yet to be written. Excessive reliance has been placed upon autobiographical writings. Two useful biographies, however, have appeared recently, Peter Lyon's *Success Story* (New York, 1963), a biography of S. S. McClure that is more accurate and written from a wider perspective than the publisher's autobiography, and Robert Bannister's *Ray Stannard Baker, the Mind and Thought of a Progressive* (New Haven and London, 1966).

Essays considering the significance of the muckrakers can be found in several general accounts of Progressivism. An analysis of the movement that calls attention to the need for historical reevaluation of muckraking is found in Richard

Hofstadter's *Age of Reform* (New York, 1955), pp. 185–212. Useful also is the discussion of muckraking found in Lloyd Morris, *Postscript to Yesterday* (New York, 1947), pp. 278–310. An appraisal that focuses on the shortcomings of the movement is found in John Chamberlain's *Farewell to Reform* (New York, 1932; paperback edition 1965), pp. 119–143.

In recent years several muckraking classics have been reissued in paperback editions. Especially significant are Ida Tarbell's *The History of the Standard Oil Company*, edited by David Chalmers (New York, 1966), Lincoln Steffens' *Shame of the Cities* (New York, 1957), and David Graham Phillips' account of Congressional corruption, *The Treason of the Senate*, edited by George E. Mowry and Judson A. Grenier (Chicago, 1964). A pioneer work in focusing national attention upon the status of the Negro is Ray Stannard Baker's *Following the Color Line*, with an introduction by Dewey Grantham (New York, 1964). Available also is Henry Demarest Lloyd's *Wealth against Commonwealth*, with an introduction by Thomas C. Cochran (Englewood Cliffs, N. J., 1963).

There is considerable literature available concerning the career of Lincoln Steffens. An interesting biographical essay is found in Charles Madison *Critics and Crusaders* (New York, 1947). Useful for an understanding of Steffens' muckraking years, although mainly concerned with placing him in the tradition of cultural radicalism, is the chapter devoted to Steffens in Christopher Lasch' *The New Radicalism in America, 1889–1963* (New York, 1965). Two article that offer a more critical view of Steffen are Granville Hicks, "Lincoln Steffens He Covered the Future" *Commentary* XIII (February 1952), pp. 147–155 and Alfred B. Rollins, "The Heart of Lincoln Steffens," *South Atlantic Quarterly* (Spring 1960), pp. 239–250.

Several journal articles are available that thoughtfully consider aspects of the muckraking movement. Two articles by David Chalmers are recommended "The Muckrakers and the Growth of Corporate Power," *American Journal of Economics and Sociology* (April 1959) pp. 295–311, and "Ray Stannard Baker's Search for Reform," *Journal of the History of Ideas*, XIX (June 1958), pp. 422–434. For a critical discussion of John Chamberlain's evaluation of the reform movement, see Louis Filler, "John Chamberlain and American Liberalism," *Colorado Quarterly*, VI (Autumn 1957), pp 200–211.